The Athlete's Guide To
Competing With
Confidence

When the stakes are high
and opponents are formidable,
those who compel their minds
to dismiss doubt and draw on
success leave the competition
victorious.

DEDICATION

To my first genuine coach and mentor, who for years patiently taught me many of the methods and techniques that are presented in the following pages—experiences and skills that provided more than just a solid foundation for my sports career—I dedicate the 2nd editions of the *WinningSTATE® Sports Confidence Series* to him.

Additionally, to *all* of the coaches who unselfishly and tirelessly help others get ahead in sports and life, *thank you!*

"Steve Knight is one of the few American Powerlifters who displays the mental control and confidence of the European Olympic Lifters."

Bill Starr, Author
Defying Gravity: How To Win At Weightlifting
The Strongest Shall Survive: Strength Training for Football

Front Cover: Rickie Fowler. AP Photo
Back Cover: Photograph by *Trevor Brown, Jr./NCAA Photos*

The information contained in this book is from the author's personal experience and is not intended to replace medical advice. Use of the information provided is at the sole choice and risk of the reader.

Library of Congress Catalog Control Number: 2010903226
Publisher's Cataloging-in-Publication (By Let's Win! International).

Let's Win! ® International, Portland, OR 97201
Mental Toughness Training 2.0

WinningSTATE ® 2–MEN'S GOLF: The Athlete's Guide to Competing with Confidence / by Steve Knight—2nd ed.
p. cm.
ISBN: 978-0-9778658-9-5
1. Sports 2. Psychology 3. Men's Golf
1. Knight, Steve ll. Title. 9 8 7 6 5 4 3 2

PRINTED IN THE UNITED STATES OF AMERICA

ACKNOWLEDGEMENTS

Many people contributed to *WinningSTATE2—MEN'S GOLF* and I am happy to acknowledge their help and thank them here.

Indirectly, Steve Krug, "Don't Make Me Think," gave us the muddle and test frame we use for more than just our website; Scott McCloud, "Understanding Comics," provided us with the fundamentals for sequential art storytelling; and Phil Knight, who during an interview jokingly commented that Coach Bowerman was a "professor of competitive response," which stimulated an "ah-ha" moment that gave us "primal competitive response" (PCR), the floor under Let's Win! Mental Toughness Training.

Then there are the artists who brought our concepts to life: Jason Cheeseman-Meyer, the best penciler around; Chris Horn, inker extraordinaire; and Dan Jackson, a fabulous painter.

Now, to those in the kitchen with their hands in the soup: to Martin and Lilly at Copyman Press, who consistently provide us top-quality printing; to Leah Sims and Vinnie Kinsella of Declaration Editing, who gave us absolutely pristine text; to Bo Johnson of Bowler Hat Comics, who helped us think of storytelling in a visual way; and Layne Ross, who pushed through seventy key language drafts and hours of banter to help shape our delivery.

To Peter McKittrick, whose "gut" reactions and direct challenge, at pivotal points, changed our direction and the "technology;" to Casey Cox, whose contribution to "the system" was significant; and to Nick Gilardi, who had an amazing impact on both the book and website during the last weeks of development. Thanks to you all!

And to Nick Bahr, whose contribution is in a category by itself; it's so broad and deep that it's almost funny trying to express my thanks in a few sentences. Nick's fingerprints are all over the following pages: his creative involvement and volume of work within several departments, year after year, have undoubtedly made the *WinningSTATE®* 2nd editions, and the Let's Win! Mental Toughness Training much more tangible products. Thanks for *all* that you do.

Finally, I am deeply grateful to those who patiently guide and mentor me as I bumble through life's steady stream of decisions.

TABLE OF CONTENTS

EXECUTE UNDER PRESSURE

INTRODUCTION

READ THIS FIRST

The biggest problem in sports is choking under pressure—submitting to the nervousness of having all eyes on you in a competitive, unfriendly, threatening environment.

This book is the first to make available "LIVE" mental toughness skills to replace doubt with confidence. In-the-trenches skills and routines to maintain emotional balance; skills to successfully battle the natural ups and downs of insecurity and self-doubt; skills to *let your "Big Dog" out* in the heat of the moment and deliver clutch performances.

Let me ask you, what's the point of developing high-level physical skills if you're a mentally weak competitor? It's pointless, unless practice is the only reason you're out for the sport, which I doubt is the case for most of you. Most of you want to compete and win. Who wants to spend years perfecting a swing on the driving range only to melt down on a playoff hole?

To win tournaments, to be a champion at any level, you need two sets of skills: the physical skills of your sport and the mental-toughness skills of a competitor. It's like a high-performance motorcycle that is useless if the driver's afraid of it; it takes a fast bike and a mentally competent driver to win races, not just a fast bike.

Consider this: How many high-level sports experts have you heard say "competing is 90% mental" or some version of "competing is all in your head"? Countless, no doubt. Pause briefly and think of a mental skill. Seriously, think of a teachable mental skill you use in competition or one you have heard a professional talk about using. Can you? Bet not.

I'm not talking about a concept, like concentration or focus, or even a pre-shot routine that is primarily physical. I'm referring to a skill similar to working the ball, like hitting a draw, fade, flop, or bump and run. Each of those swings has a teachable, step-by-step skill process for executing that shot. Go ahead, name a *mental skill*.

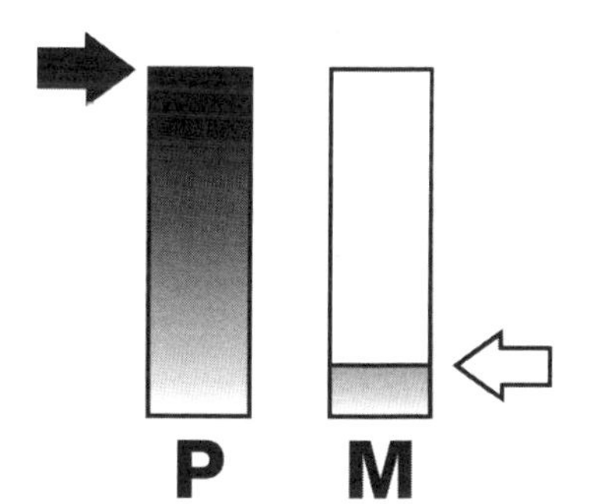

The Skills Comparison diagram (left) highlights the typical imbalance between many athletes' physical and mental skill levels. Excellent physical skills alone are great, if practice is the only reason you're out for the sport.

Seems like a serious disconnect to me. If sports are about competing and winning, and if competing is 90% mental, where are the skills?

I assume you agree that a mental approach to competition is needed, so the next step is clearing the clutter of misinformation with new, simple ideas about how to build reliable competition confidence.

Within the following chapters are "squash-the-bug" skills and routines to take your mental preparation to the next level—a level that produces more gratifying performances. Performances when you'll be able to face the pressure and not flinch. Performances when the final putt is made you'll be able to *truthfully* say to yourself, "I didn't choke; I gave it all I had." You accomplish that *mentally*.

The Problem

The problem is, if you're among the majority of athletes and coaches who believe competition confidence lives in hard work, I'm afraid you're going to be working for a long time without finding what you're working for. It's the most common misunderstanding in competitive sports and one of the myths I plan on busting: the myth that hard physical work automatically translates into competition confidence.

For example, soon after we introduced *WinningSTATE—BASEBALL* in 2003, a batting coach requested the names of our expert hitters, because if we weren't expert hitters, how could we talk about hitting with confidence, let alone teach it. Since then we have received numerous requests with similarly framed questions. They all link competition confidence to expert physical skills and hard physical work. This clearly illustrates the broad confusion and misinformation associated with how emotional pressure is actually managed when it's showtime.

Perspective is the issue. Confidence under pressure has little to do with the physical skills of a sport—any sport. Yes, an argument can be made that the more skilled athletes are physically, the more confident they will be under pressure. But when you really think about it, that's a limited view of where competition confidence lives, an address where you know you will always find it—always.

Competition confidence lives in mental toughness. Believing you can make the swing and then having the assertiveness to step up and say "watch this" and actually do it.

Most of you don't think like that. Performing under pressure requires a mental skillset that switches your core feeling from friendly and agreeable to challenging and assertive—a *selfish* mentality. For many, possibly even you, that deep change from passive and respectful to assertive and confrontational presents a significant mental challenge.

Selfish? Assertive? Confrontational? Yes! Absolutely—no question! We will talk a lot about being selfish, assertive, confrontational, daring, and bold in the coming chapters.

Back to myth busting—hard physical work alone is not going to eliminate timidity, dwelling on negativity, and surrendering to doubt. Has it yet? It never will. It helps increase believing a little, but it will never provide Big Dog confidence when it's showtime.

What's missing? *Perspective.* Confidence lives in emotion, not swing skills. Emotion: That weird, slippery world of feelings.

The issue with perspective is that we utterly fail to recognize the distinct difference between practice confidence and competition confidence. Like oil and water, the two are drastically different elements. Practice emotions are calmer and safer than competition emotions, which are often violent and negative.

The key point is this: As competitors, we literally live in two radically different worlds and we must know how to *switch* from one world to the other with ease.

The DNA illustration (above) represents the idea that competition confidence comes from genetics and physical traits. We disagree. We believe competition confidence comes from managing super emotions, not genes. Emotions: that weird slippery world of feelings and primal reactions.

This contrast between practice and competition is vital. Draw a thick black line between the two. Practice is learn-time. Competition is showtime. Practice is safe, because that's where mistakes are supposed to be made. The lack of pressure helps most athletes perform better. But, who has ever made it to the next level based on his practice videos?

Our Theory

The Let's Win! confidence theory is simple: Confidence comes from direct experiences and learned skills, not genetic traits. Along with busting the "physical work will make you confident" myth, I'm also going to expose "trait theory."

In case the term "trait" is unclear, our traits are directly connected to our genetics. The color of our eyes, our height, and our quickness are determined by our genes, along with most everything else that make us who we are. Our traits come from our genes.

Trait theory suggests that the level of our confidence is determined by our parents, who either pass along the confidence gene or they don't. Sorry. To suggest that we are either born with confidence or we're not is missing the obvious. We gain and lose confidence in a millisecond. A trait is consistent; it does not change due to mood swings. In other words, under pressure our eyes aren't blue one minute and brown the next. Therefore, confidence is an attitude to be gained through experiences and skills, not genetic traits.

To explain further, competition confidence lives in overcoming "I can't" thinking—the natural first tendency for most of us. Most of us think, feel, and believe "I can't" as opposed to "I can." Most of us are controlled by an unshakeable fear of failure. And because of this we must be able to *override* that deep-seated self-doubt. We do this by expanding our perspective and working on the mental toughness skills to overcome "I can't" thinking and feelings. We can actually grow our confidence.

Henry Ford put it well: "Whether you think you can or you can't, you're probably right."

Our theory, if you buy into it, is a perspective changer. The power of your thoughts is unavoidable. Attacking the ball and not yourself is how to compete and win. You do that first by realizing you have the power *right now* to dismiss doubt and to believe in your physical abilities. The science supports our theory.

The Science

Recently we were digging around looking for scientific findings to support our experience/skill-based confidence theory, and we uncovered several compelling bits of evidence.

This won't be too technical.

The primary part of our brain that is responsible for certain emotional reactions, fear in particular, is the amygdala (a-mig-da-la). We refer to the amygdala as our "emotional brain" throughout the book.

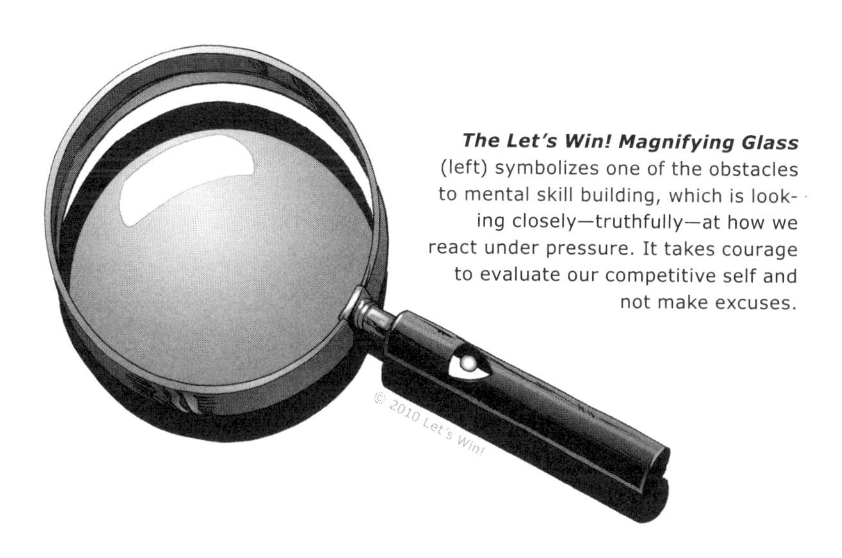

The Let's Win! Magnifying Glass (left) symbolizes one of the obstacles to mental skill building, which is looking closely—truthfully—at how we react under pressure. It takes courage to evaluate our competitive self and not make excuses.

Our emotional brain is both our friend and our enemy. It controls our fight-or-flight response. Actually, there is a third response, the deer-in-the-headlights reaction: to freeze. Through these three responses, our emotional brain attempts to protect us from physical and social danger; it's sort of an auto response to threat.

Hang with me here—this is a fun realization. It opens the doors to understanding why we behave the way we do.

For example, think of when someone leaps out from behind something and scares us. Our eyes widen, our heart rate leaps, and we *feel* scared. Why? Because we're gonna get eaten. In a split second we have to make the 3F decision: to fight, flee, or freeze. That's why we get so mad; we have a physical reaction to getting scared. We have no choice. Way back when, that adrenaline rush helped us run and climb faster than the claws and teeth that were inches behind us. That physical self-preservation reaction is controlled by our emotional brain, and our emotional brain protects us from perceived social danger in the same way.

To easily prove the point, it's commonly known that peoples' number one fear is speaking in public. No claws or teeth in that social scene, but the self-preservation reaction is just as strong. It's similar in every way: increased heart rate, dry mouth, confusion, the shakes, etc. Why? Speaking in public (e.g., giving a class presentation) is threatening, and our emotional brain freaks out. We don't want to look bad, but we believe that we probably will look bad, so we want out of there fast. Reactions from both physical and social threats are forms of self-preservation, which is obviously a good thing, but as competitors we must harness that nervous competitive energy or it becomes overwhelming and inhibits rather than enhances. Translation: We choke rather than post a personal best.

To melt down or not to melt down, that *is* the ongoing question.

The meltdown reaction is to freak out and crash, compared to the prepared reaction which is to freak out, *think,* and positively respond. One is pure Monkey Mode and the other is managed with emotional intelligence supported by *rehearsed* mental skills and routines.

Monkey Mode vs. Competition Mindset—one is unrestrained emotional chaos, and the other is disciplined, focused, and balanced.

The core of a competition mindset is emotional intelligence, which allows us to be present during the emotional drama and not mentally check out—to openly realize we're emotionally reacting, know why we're reacting, and then effectively manage the reaction. Monkey Mode, on the other hand, is an unrestrained emotional meltdown. Can't you see it? When monkeys are excited, for whatever reason, they freak out. They chatter, scream, run, climb, and flail their arms all about. Even though we humans may not show the drama outwardly, inside very few of us have learned to manage intense emotional conflict. We typically succumb to irrational "what if" Monkey Mode nonsense.

"What if I yank it OB," "What if I miss it right," "What if I'm too quick at the top," and "What if he outdrives me," are all an unprepared competitor's negative reactions to social threat stimuli, reactions that center in a feeling of "I'm inadequate." (Be sure to say that with a high, whiny, weak voice.)

Why am I coming down so hard on this? As competitors wanting to deliver our best at the big show, we don't have the luxury of uncontrolled emotional outbursts. They are our undoing.

For now, realize that when you want it bad and the competition is good you will always have severe self-doubt reactions, maybe several hundred per round. So if you're going to be persistently faced, shot after shot, with 3F decisions (to fight, flee, or freeze), why not *plan and prepare?* When you do you'll be able to *react and use* that highly charged, volatile, amazing competition energy.

Having fun under the lights, stepping up and facing the Doubt Demons in the heat of the moment, and either crashing or pulling it off, is why I compete. Why do you compete?

The Approach

Just like there are a variety of personalities, there are endless approaches to building and using LIVE mental skills, because we all learn so differently. But just as the physical fundamentals of a solid swing are similar for everyone, the fundamentals of building mental skills are also very similar. Brace yourself, it starts with honest self-reflection.

> ***As competitors wanting to deliver our best at the big show, we don't have the luxury of uncontrolled emotional outbursts. They are our undoing.***

Yikes! This is when many people plug their ears, cover their eyes, and run out of the room. Having rational, emotionally intelligent conversations with ourselves can be threatening, at first, until we experience the personal power that is gained from simple reflection.

The approach begins with intelligent reflection, which helps us understand our true competitive orientation, actual experiences, and the typical way we respond to threatening situations of any kind. We call this normal reaction to threat our "primal competitive response." Consider this: Don't we first need to evaluate what needs improving, before we can improve it?

When we have the courage to look inside and accurately view our "competitive self," this typically produces an immediate response that is something like, "I'm mentally tougher than I thought." And with that core ah-ha moment, it's game on. We're then able to construct a plan to improve, just like analyzing and adapting swing changes and course strategies.

The Plan

The plan is to increase your ability to *talk and think* about your competitive self, and then to equip yourself with usable mental skills that override negative emotions. The plan is to assemble the skills to stay mentally tough under a barrage of doubt and uncertainty, to be able to push forward toward what you want, whatever that may be.

If you are open, engaged, and willing to see how your competitive core works, when you put this book down you will have a greater understanding of how to increase *your* competition confidence. As a bonus, deliberate mental-skill-building will affect more than just your golf performance; it will also positively affect many aspects of your life, for the rest of your life.

The Skills and Routines

There are numerous new skills and routines in the following chapters to increase your *competition confidence* right now, to take your mental game to the next level. An important first realization is grasping that you already have *it;* you definitely have what it takes. And if you tackle mental-skill-building with just a little passion, in no time you'll have greater control over your competitive emotions when the expectations are huge and everyone is focused on you. You'll have a process to maintain emotional stability as the pressure level rises.

Remember, we all have a Big Dog deep inside of us, our mentally tough "OtherSelf" who can face tough challenges and boldly execute under the greatest of pressure. So believe and let your Big Dog out!

Inside every one of us is a Little Dog and a Big Dog:

Our Little Dog Self:

Our Little Dog self is mentally unprepared for competition and gets overwhelmed by distractions and formidable opponents. Under pressure, our Little Dog self fears the spotlight, can't think, becomes emotionally disoriented, and melts under the lights.

Our Big Dog Self:

Our Big Dog self is mentally well prepared for competition and can easily switch from friendly and agreeable to challenging and assertive. Under pressure, our Big Dog self has the skills to welcome the spotlight, think objectively, *draw on success*, and boldly execute.

LET YOUR BIG DOG OUT!

CHAPTER 1

SWITCH

A **Competition** Mindset

In this chapter you will learn how to *switch*—mental toughness skill #1—a competition skill that deliberately changes our attitude from nice to confrontational. Competition demands it; there is no room for friendliness.

Our Big Dog self
can *switch* attitudes from friendly
and agreeable to challenging
and assertive.

You've played for years. You work hard at practice. Your golf skills are sharp and you know what you're capable of. You've dreamed about rising above the competition at state with a bogie-free round or sticking a long iron on the 18th to seal the team win. But instead, when the pressure was on, you yanked one OB or fanned a dead-straight, uphill three-footer. Too many times you've walked off the course feeling disappointed and dejected. You wonder what's missing. You wonder why you struggle with pulling off key shots when you need them most. You wonder why the last tournament of the season has never been your best. You wonder how to take your tournament play to a winning level. Answer: It's time to learn how to compete—*mentally*.

Tournament competition is entirely unlike practice: The expectations, the excitement, the opponents you've never faced before, along with demanding coaches and freaked-out teammates, all combine to create an extraordinary environment that requires a second set of skills just to survive, let alone to succeed. Add tremendous pressure to win from all directions and it becomes crystal clear that the second set of skills required is a set of mental toughness skills—skills that must be developed to the point of being second nature, just like driving, chipping, flopping, and putting.

The illustration on the next page amplifies that idea. That we must have the skills to deliberately separate our everyday social life from the emotionally turbulent world of competing—a threatening world that routinely sucks the oxygen out of many great athletes.

Think about it. Typically our social life is soft, fluffy, and relaxed, as opposed to competing which is harsh, rough, and intense. One is ordinary, where the other is extraordinary. One is safe, where the other is threatening. Being able to deliberately *switch* our attitude from courteous to confrontational is the first mental skill required to overcome the nerves, to let our Big Dogs out, and to boldly execute.

Before I breakdown the switch skill further, into understandable parts, I need to introduce your real opponent: the 3 Doubt Demons.

The 3 Doubt Demons

They are relentless. Facing them is a never-ending battle. The majority of us, no matter how mentally skilled we become, are never free of the 3 Doubt Demons. We battle their constant negativity our entire lives—it's just the way we're programmed.

The 3 Doubt Demons intimately know our deepest fears and inhibitions, and constantly project negative outcomes. The Demon of Inadequacy, the Demon of Past Failure, and the Demon of Embarrassment plot and plan to make us feel small, fearful, and intimidated. Weird isn't it? Why are we so fearful? Why are we so self-defeating? And it's all in our heads.

Be aware that the 3 Doubt Demons give us the hardest time during the transitions. For example, when we're en route to a tournament we might have some butterflies, but as we walk onto the range our right brain erupts and the Doubt Demons launch an attack. The Demon of Inadequacy presents mental images of our weaknesses, the Demon of Past Failure reminds us of not-so-great past performances, and the Demon of Embarrassment projects thoughts and feelings of potential humiliation.

Emotional transitions are when the Doubt Demons talk us out of what we can do and into what we can't do. Emotional transitions are when most of us go nuts, melt down emotionally, and spiral into full-on Monkey Mode. To mount an effective counter attack, we must know how to successfully manage the many emotional transitions we go through each and every round.

Example: The time between warm-ups and sticking the first peg in the ground is a transition when we can easily go from savoring the competitive moment and getting pumped up about competing to emotionally buying into the negative drama, crashing under the pressure to perform, and getting off to a rocky start. In order to shift from one mental/emotional state to another, we must purposefully *switch attitudes* during emotional transitions. In golf, that happens at least seventy times.

We'll talk more about the 3 Doubt Demons in the coming chapters, but for now realize that under pressure they are what gets in our way. To be successful we must know how to better manage nervy, must-make transitions by switching to a competition mindset.

The Competition Gate (right) exaggerates the psychological intimidation many of us feel when entering competitive environments. We turn simple sports venues into looming, intimidating monsters ... and it's all in our heads.

COMPETITION

Switch: A Competition Mindset

If you are a friendly, nice, giving person, you must radically alter your attitude to handle the emotional drama before and during competitions. Why? Competing is not about being friendly, nice, and giving. Competing at its very core is about being challenging and taking. There's only one trophy and you must take it—it will never be handed to you. Permission is not required, nor will it ever be given. To be successful in competitive sports you must know how to switch to a challenging, assertive, taker mindset—a *competition mindset*.

Look closely at *Rational vs. Emotional* on pages 16 and 17. Read the captions. Those two conflicting images tie directly to the switch skill and the underlying theme of this book, which is to help you develop the skills to lessen the intensity of your right brain by increasing the dominance of your left brain, to be less emotional and more rational under pressure. We call this the LBi Technique, a left brain integration technique we use to switch from courteous to confrontational and from emotional to rational. When our rational (left brain) competition mindset has the loudest voice, the 3 Doubt Demons don't stand a chance.

I need to interrupt the flow for a minute to make a right brain/left brain disclaimer. Many experts in the field of neuroscience (brain science) express disdain for the supposed left brain/right brain theory, which claims that the left hemisphere is where logic takes place (map reading, math calculations, engineering, structure, etc.), while the right hemisphere is random, creative, imaginative, and emotional. The experts claim that the right/left theory is over-simplified and that the brain is much more complicated. Okay. The point of utilizing the two-brain concept is not to promote whether the left/right theory is scientifically factual, but rather to illustrate the point that logic is linked to Big Dog "bring it" execution, while emotion is linked to Little Dog "I can't" melting. But more importantly, we can influence which brain we listen to; by being mentally equipped, we can influence how we respond to heightened emotions, either negatively or positively.

Regardless of the geography of the brain and how it functions, left side, right side, or a combination, no one can deny that our brains operate in two distinct ways, rationally and emotionally. The question for you to consider is this: When confronted with an emotional challenge, which one of your brains has the loudest voice?

Back to switch. It's such a key skill it deserves further explanation to make sure its taker mentality is not misunderstood.

For example, wanting it is not the same as taking it. Many of your coaches may have talked about "wanting it," attempting to help grow the competitive fire in your belly. But wanting it does not create action. Wanting it may help us get emotionally fired up, but executing requires action. When there's a limited supply of food on the table and there are a lot of people who need to eat, you might want the food on the table, but if you're uncomfortable with grabbing the food first and not sharing, you will always struggle with competing, always.

For many of you this is a mind bender, because being a *taker* is a foreign concept. Taking does not fit into your social perspective. However, if you really think about it, competing requires a taker mentality if you're going to win.

Are you seeing the connection? In competition, it's okay not to share. Actually, sharing is impossible.

The obstacle to embracing this taker perspective is overcoming social conditioning—how we were raised. Most of us were conditioned from birth to always share, to be modest, gentle, kindhearted and compassionate, and to not be a showoff. Those attitudes are the absolute opposite of what is needed to be successful in any competitive environment. It's just the way it is.

The *Switch* illustration on page 19 attempts to make this black-and-white contrast clear. Notice the expression difference. Compare the descriptions. Do you identify with bold, assertive, and selfish? Or do you identify more with modest, agreeable, and giving?

"I was competitive in whatever I did. You have to be a competitor. You can't be soft."

~Jack Nicklaus~

In competition, our *left brain* reacts to heightened emotions with a balanced mindset; it rationally sorts through the nonsense, makes crisp decisions, is rock solid, and executes with confidence.

Yes, this is a mind bender. However, a taker mentality is at the core of every successful competitor. Competitors think "It is mine, get out of my way, I'm taking it!" A real competition takes place when more than one athlete/competitor has this taker mentality and can back it up with physical skills. Then we have a real, head-to-head, nose-to-nose, intense competition.

The main idea of the switch skill is to get you over your social niceness, so you can actually compete, not just participate. If this taker mentality is

In competition, our *right brain* reacts to heightened emotions with a Monkey Mode mindset; it streams one irrational, illogical thought after another, becomes disoriented, and melts down.

just too far outside your comfort zone, if it's just too hard to relate to, than try developing a "defensive" switch attitude—find your bone.

Picture a dog chewing on a bone while another dog approaches and attempts to take the bone. I don't think so. The dog with the bone will defend its treasure with all its might. Where's *your* bone? What will *you* defend? Anything? Are you mostly timid and submissive or will you stand your ground and fight back? What's inside you? Where's your fire? What will you fight for? Guaranteed, you have more fire than you realize, you just don't think about your competitive fire, your Grr factor, and how to use it. Hopefully, we're going to change that.

In pressure situations, we all have an emotional response spectrum, from negative to positive, which the *Grr Meter* illustrates on the next page. Where do your emotional responses fit on the Grr Meter? Think about it.

We will talk a lot about our Grr factor—our fight back power—in the coming chapters; too much Grr is just as detrimental as too little Grr. At this point, realize that emotions must be managed in competition and switching from emotional to rational is the first skill to being able to do that.

In case the defensive switch perspective is easier to relate to, here's another example, siblings. It doesn't matter whether they are younger or older, male or female, all siblings are pains at some point. They take our stuff and cause us endless problems and frustration, just as we do them. But, we have no problem chasing them down the hall and getting our stuff back—we will defend our territory. True? The point is that you have more Grr (fight) in you than you realize, so get okay with letting it out in competition and using it to your advantage.

Don't misunderstand this sibling example; I'm not suggesting that many of you don't have wonderful relationships with your brothers and sisters. That's not the point. No matter how wonderful our relationships, if they take our stuff without permission, they're going to pay, one way or another. We won't hesitate. Why? Because we don't care if they like it or not, they have violated our space and taken our stuff, so it's payback time—period. The point is, we take action, we fight back, we don't flee or freeze. We defend our territory with little regard for social consequences. We fight with siblings from birth. It's just the way it is.

Think about switching to your OtherSelf, either to a taker or a defender. Try to create a counter argument that switching is not required. You can't. Switching to a combative, challenging, "it's mine" competitive attitude is essential. You must be able to assert your will, whether it's through a taker or defender perspective, and *grab the prize* or the competition will.

I know this makes sense to you; now the real task is learning how to translate it into action, how to do it. That's what the rest of the Let's Win! mental toughness skills will help you do: narrow, fuel, override, replace, believe, and dream. For now, realize that switching from friendly to challenging is mandatory, so figure out what kind of mental switching

SWITCH

MENTAL SKILL #1: Turn on your OtherSelf.

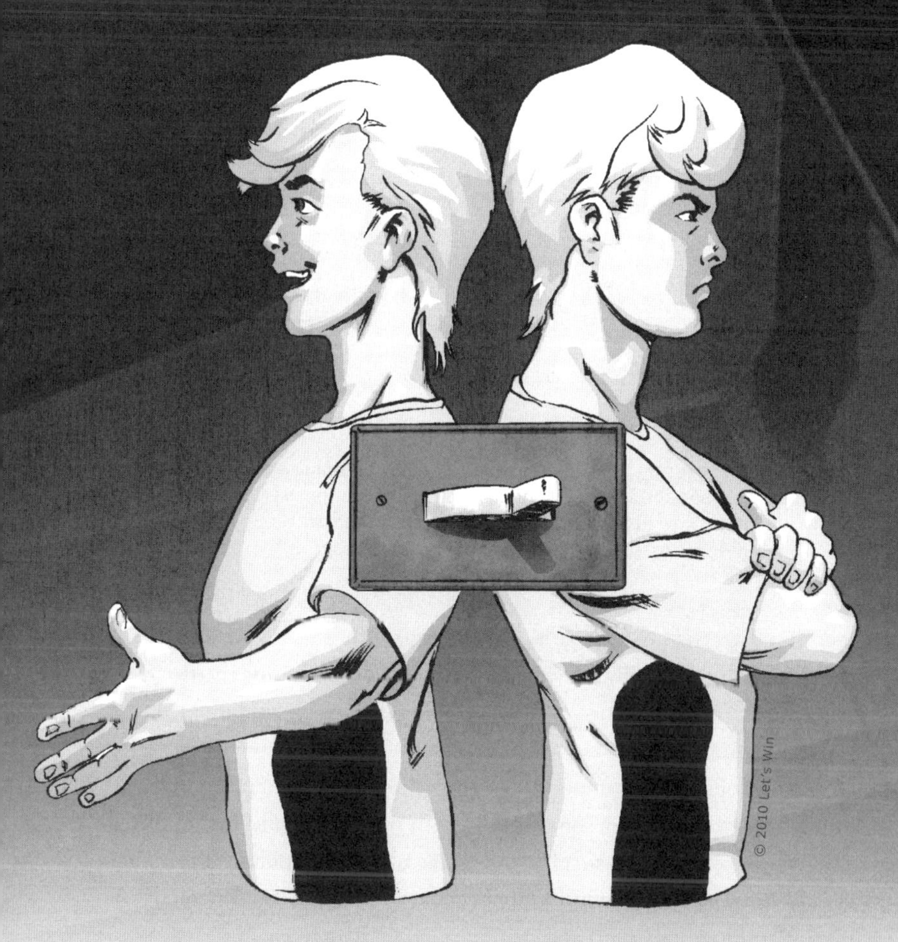

FRIENDLY MODE	COMPETITION MODE
Modest ○	• Bold
Agreeable ○	• Assertive
Giving ○	• Selfish

Switch—mental skill #1 (above). Competitions require that you take the prize, so switch attitudes and compete, to win. Switch to your *OtherSelf*, your mentally tough, Big Dog self who is not held back by social conditioning.

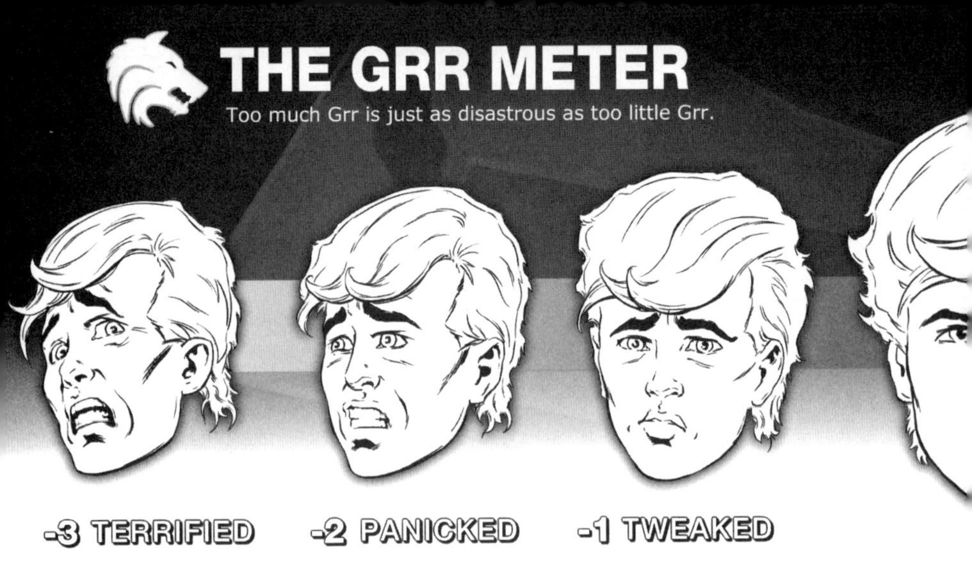

The Grr Meter (above) shows our emotional response spectrum to physical and social challenges (threats). Mentally competent, complete athletes float between -1 and +1. Above or below has proven to decrease success. Too much Grr is just as disastrous as too little Grr.

technique works best for you. Create your OtherSelf, your competitive self. The self what will bravely step up and defend your territory, your stuff, and your competitive reputation. You have to, no one else can or will ... it's up to you.

Remember, when competing we must transition from one world to another, a mental zone for some that is both unfamiliar and uncomfortable. The attitude required to survive and thrive in that threatening environment is *focused seriousness*—a mindset that is not too common today, which is why it's difficult to understand and do.

Focused Seriousness

For many young athletes, seriousness means being angry or overly emotional, the fuming end of the Grr Meter. But that's not it. Seriousness is about a balanced, focused determination, being able to concentrate and use the intense competition emotions to your advantage—fighting for the bone. This is what separates true competitors from the majority of athletes who only want to *participate* in sports. Making faces and trying to look all focused and Grred up is not being serious, it's just posturing. Clutch competitors don't *act* serious—they're either serious or they're not.

Check out the *The Complete Athlete* illustration on the next page. Will strength, speed, and conditioning give you focused seriousness under pressure? No, they won't. It's mental.

Focused seriousness comes from attitude, not anger. No acting, no pretending, no faking; it's steely-eyed, piercing concentration. We block out everything except the objective, being completely in the moment, not lost in emotional anxiety and self-doubt. Focused seriousness comes from a taker or defender attitude.

Here's what focused seriousness is not: It's not saying to yourself, "I want it, I want it, I want it," or "I can, I can, I can." That's emotional. Of course you want it and of course you can. Seriousness is not repeating positive statements or *imagining* success. Seriousness *is* execution and nothing else, because executing on demand is what separates champions from contenders.

Champions (Big Dog competitors) command a competition mindset that is pure seriousness. They can *switch* from friendly to challenging, from agreeable to confrontational. They realize that a serious, assertive mindset is an absolute necessity to performing their best.

Before I close this chapter on the switch skill, I need to bust another myth, the peak performer myth.

The Peak Performer Myth

Realize your potential! Be all that you can be! Take it to the limit! Go for the glory! Be a peak performer! Yikes! All of that sounds good and may be a little bit motivating, but how is attempting to pump you up to realize your potential going to help you actually defeat the Doubt Demons when it's all on the line and your mind is confused, distracted, and disoriented? It can't, it doesn't, and it won't for the majority of you.

Many of your coaches may have given one version or another of the peak performer motivation speech. While they mean well, that speech typically falls on deaf ears. Don't get me wrong, all of that life achievement stuff is great, but it is way off point when it comes to building and controlling confidence under pressures. A more functional, sink-your-teeth-into-it approach is needed.

Researchers are to blame. It all started back in the day when psychologists wanted to understand why one person performs better than another under pressure. Those early researchers thought that analyzing national and Olympic champions would shed some light on the topic. Guess what they found out? National and Olympic champions push themselves to their limits, giving it all they've got. (Duh.) They labeled those individuals "peak performers" and everyone else "underachievers." Talk about not seeing the forest through the trees. Trust me guys, I've known lots of world-class competitors who push themselves to their limits, yet still emotionally crash under the lights.

Managing intense emotions under pressure has little to do with being a person who is striving to be an elite athlete—a peak performer. Additionally, being labeled an underachiever unless you're pursuing some kind of world-level competition is ridiculous.

Realize that you don't have to be an elite athlete or intensely desire the spotlight to succeed in competition. You simply have to know how to switch attitudes and manage your emotions by *thinking rationally* and drawing on previous success.

That's how to succeed under pressure, being able to think, which has nothing to do with your motivation level. If you also have the daily drive and desire to push yourself to be all that you can be, to be an elite athlete/competitor, to be a state, national, or world champion, rock on!

But rest assured, just because you may not be a peak performer does not exclude you from being a fierce, confident competitor.

As we finish this chapter, I encourage you not to treat this information passively, but rather to engage the *idea.* At the very least, be able to explain it, because to explain it you must understand it, and if you understand it you'll be closer to being able to do it.

THE COMPLETE ATHLETE

Your mind is your most powerful weapon.

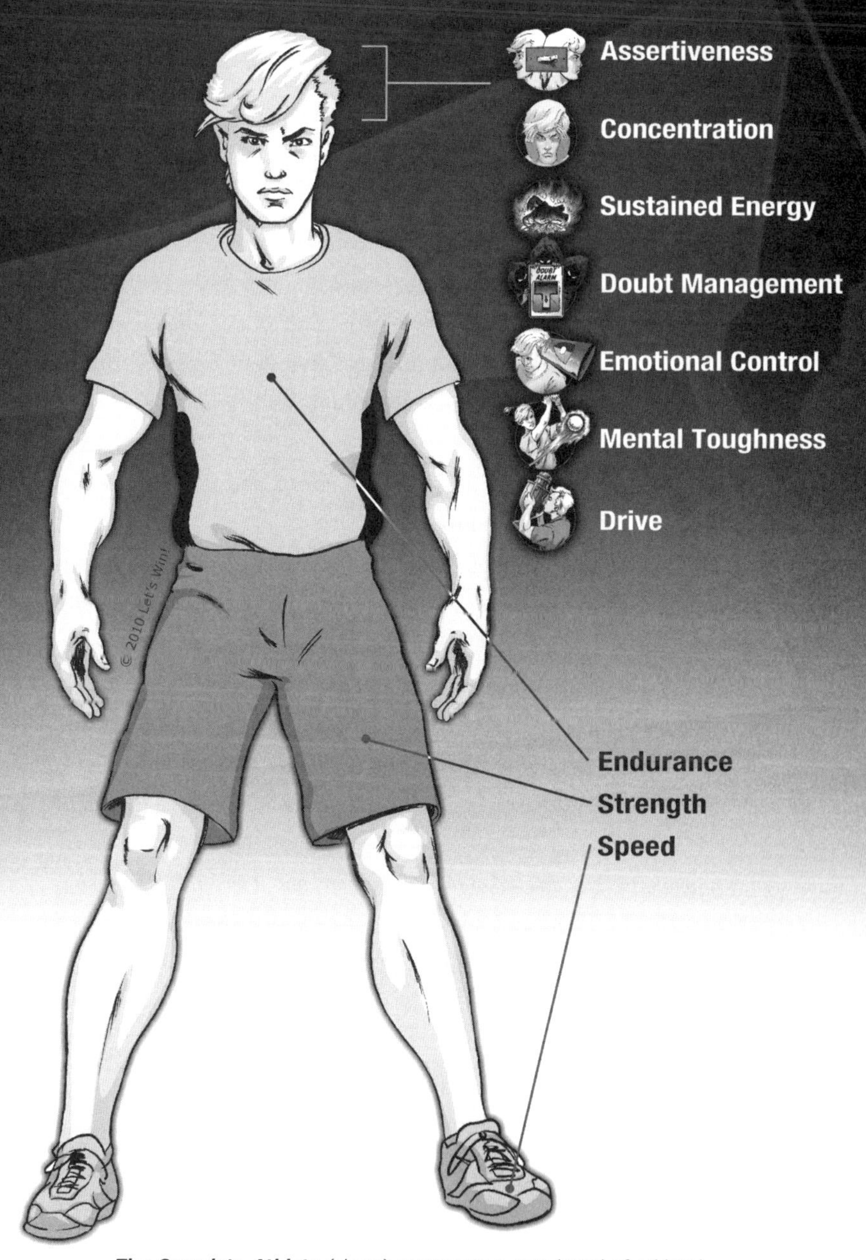

The Complete Athlete (above) represents a new breed of athlete/competitor. One who has the mental toughness skills to control his emotions under pressure and believe in himself when it's all on the line. One who can step up in the heat of the moment and deliver.

Switching to a confrontational, challenging competition mindset is essential. Assert your will and take what is rightfully yours.

Which switch concept feels better to you: Taker or defender? If neither, then come up with your own way to switch. Just be aware that the objective of switching is to create an attitude, a competitive OtherSelf that desperately needs something from the competition, something you will relentlessly compete for that both forces and enables you to execute under intense pressure.

Eventually this awareness turns into an actual skill you use to turn your competition mindset on and off, just like a light switch: click => click. And it must be that simple.

If the switch skill is still a little hazy, Chapter 2 and Chapter 4 will provide additional details and examples.

Everything in this book, every skill, routine, and illustration is presented with a single purpose in mind, to help you pull off great shots when you need them most, to help you take your mental game to a winning level.

Remember, switching to a confrontational, challenging "it's mine" competition mindset is essential. You must be able to assert your will whether it's through a taker or defender mindset and *grab the prize* or the competition will.

From The History Channel's description of the DVD series *EVOLVE*:

> *It's a tough, violent, and lethal world out there, and it's been that way since the dawn of time. Roughly 99 percent of all species have become extinct. What enabled that other one percent to survive the cutthroat competition? Their ability to.... EVOLVE.*

Now you're learning how to compete—*mentally*.

CHAPTER 1

REVIEW

Switch: A Competition Mindset

Summary

Performing in public goes against our social conditioning. From birth we're trained to be modest, to not showoff, and to be considerate, nice, and friendly. Those attitudes and associated behaviors are the absolute opposite of what is needed to succeed in competition, where we must *switch* attitudes to assertive, confrontation, and bold—*a competition mindset.*

Test—What did you learn?

True/False Statements:

1) Switching to a competition mindset is essential.
2) Successful competitors float between -1 and +1 on the Grr Meter.
3) The Doubt Demon of Fear is one of the 3 Doubt Demons.
4) Our left brain controls our emotions.

Do It!

Give yourself *permission* to be selfish. Do it! Switch from nice to confrontation (click=>click). At the very least, observe all competitively threatening situations through the switch lens. Observe who is passive, doubting, and confused and who is assertive, confident, and confrontational. *Switch*.

CHAPTER 2

NARROW

Conquer The Stadium

In this chapter you will learn how to *narrow*—mental toughness skill #2—a competition skill that forcefully narrows our concentration to only what's important: the mechanics of the shot and confidence.

Our Big Dog self
can *narrow* concentration to shot
requirements, swing keys,
and past success.

Tournaments challenge the *focus* of many athletes. Ranked opponents, intense coaches, specific procedures, changing weather conditions, and hundreds of spectators are all ingredients in the competition pressure cooker. Distractions are nonstop, and the confusion can be overwhelming.

The intensity at district, state, and national competitions takes many athletes out of their comfort zones and leaves them numb, even babbling in the corner, because they don't have a mental plan.

The constant visual distractions and overall competition commotion can cause extreme emotional instability and make for an unpredictable roller-coaster experience. Golf course chaos prevents athletes of all ages from achieving their competitive potential, because they haven't equipped themselves with the tools needed to *narrow their focus* to what's important—confidence and the mechanics of the shot.

Remember, confidence is not some genetic, mystical thing that you either have or you don't. Confidence and mental toughness live in deliberate, rational thinking, not genes.

Take a close look at the *When All Eyes Are On You* illustration on page 31. That is a golfer's extraordinary second reality as a competitor. It's like being in a fishbowl and a pressure cooker at the same time; we're surrounded and there's no way out. Our perceptions change, everything gets distorted, and it feels like everything's closing in on us. The Doubt Demons attack from all directions, using changing tournament conditions and intimate knowledge of our deepest fears to further their devious plan of convincing us that we don't have it in us, that we're going to fail. A reliable counterattack is essential.

Being able to *narrow* your concentration to shot requirements and swings keys, along with listening intently to that small voice telling you *why* you can believe in yourself, requires a series of skills and routines that all start with the switch perspective, so let's briefly revisit the *switch* skill presented in the last chapter.

Your OtherSelf

As we discussed previously, when competing we transition from a psychologically safe place to a psychologically threatening place—a mental zone that is typically uncomfortable for most. But, to succeed in this confrontational environment we must construct an "OtherSelf," a competitive self, a mentality that is not social and is okay with stepping out, tackling challenges, showing off, and winning.

It's important to realize that your OtherSelf is not a "projection." Projecting is a shallow outward fantasy of what you want everyone else to see, not a solid attitude deep inside that is pure seriousness.

For example, the attitude, and personality, you project when you're sitting at the dinner table with your family is very different from the attitude and personality you project when you're out with your friends. We control those different outward social projections whether we realize it or not. We learn how to do this very early in life. Sometimes they are sincere and sometimes they are not. Either way, social projections are based on getting a reaction out of those around us. Your competitive OtherSelf is *not* an outward social projection. Your competitive OtherSelf doesn't care who is watching or what they are thinking. Your competitive OtherSelf is only concerned with one thing: *executing.*

Weightlifters can be the worst at projecting—yelling, slapping, huffing and puffing. Do they think they're intimidating the weights? I don't think so. Or some might say, "That's what gets me up." I don't think so. In most cases it's an outward display of *fear.* They're scared to death and don't know how to channel their emotions. They release that valuable, pent-up emotional energy all over the arena, which is both rookie behavior and a tremendous energy drain.

I used to enjoy watching all those goofballs going through their displays of fear, because it gave me a competitive advantage—they were ex-

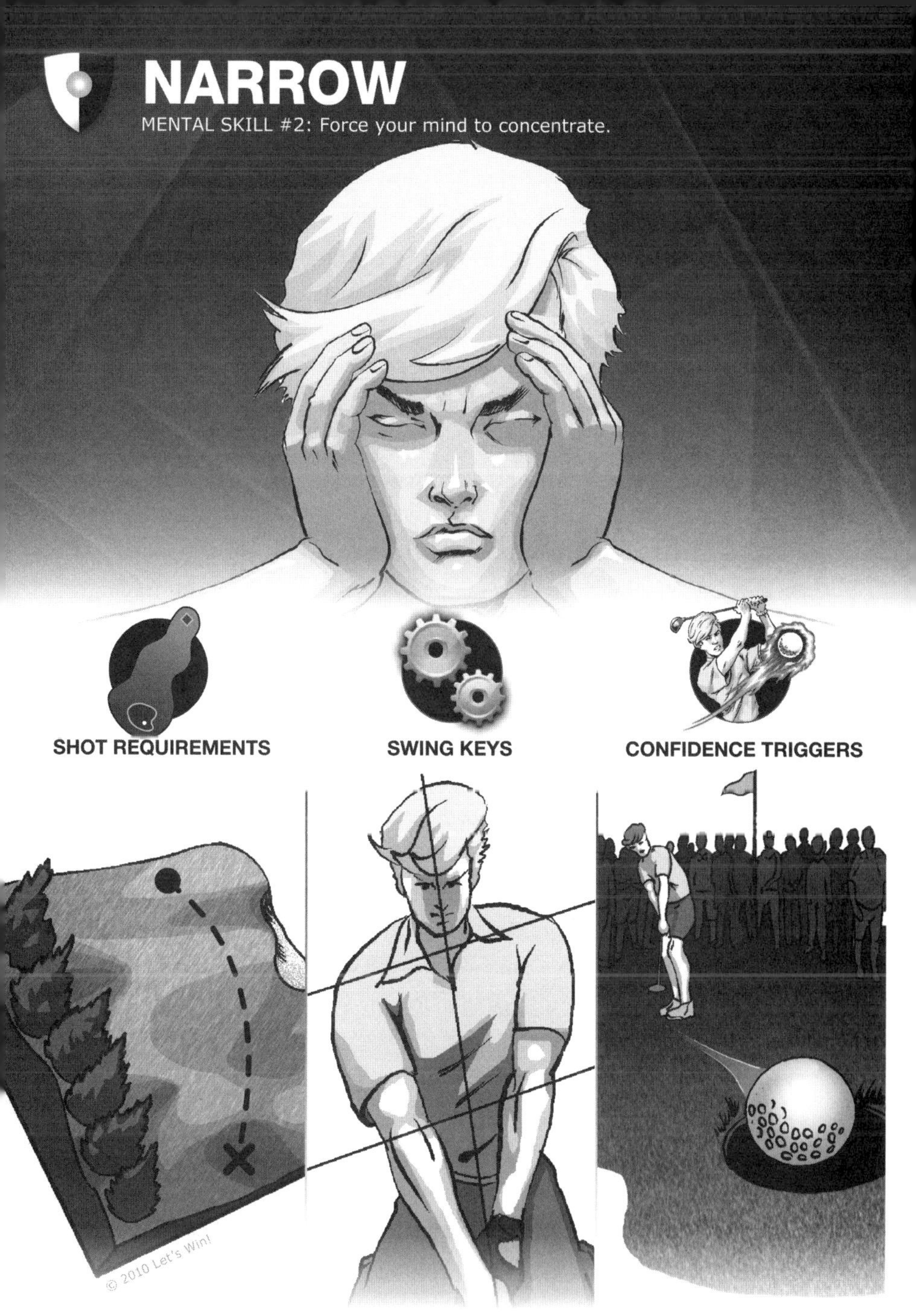

Narrow—mental skill #2 (above). Under pressure, when your mind is racing at 300 miles an hour, vigorously block out distractions by narrowing your focus to what's important: that shot's requirements, your swing keys, your confidence triggers, and nothing else.

hausting themselves. Don't project your other self, *be* your OtherSelf—a competitor. Harness and focus your emotional energy. Executing is about doing, not posturing.

Once you've learned to switch to your competitive OtherSelf, then you need simple routines that help *narrow* your concentration to the obvious: shot strategy, swing mechanics, and your confidence.

The following PRE Competition Routines and Battle Zones technique, unlike our erratic emotions, are tangible, predictable, and stable. They help reduce nerves, fight back negative thinking, and solidify our core confidence. They help us believe in our ball striking when the competition and the 3 Doubt Demons are breathing down our necks.

PRE Competition Routines

Do you *feel* what the *When All Eyes Are On You* illustration is portraying? Inside every competition venue, you are all alone. No friends, no family, no nothing. You are all by yourself—especially as golfers. Even with fellow competitors and hundreds of spectators within close proximity—you are all alone.

This is why competing is 90% mental, and why mental toughness skills are essential. They're your 15th club.

We use the PRE Competition Routines (and the associated skills) to mentally prepare for the emotional drama and doubtful thinking, which will always accompany pressure situations—always. We use these skills and routines not just before competitions, but during competitions as well.

Here are the five PRE Competition Routines:

#1 Plan:

On tournament day, especially before leaving for an away competition, planning and packing *all* of our competition necessities is critical. First, make a list—a written list. Then make sure all of your things are laid out in front of you and ready to be packed: equipment, back-up equipment, clothes, fuel, fluids, accessories, etc.

Example: If you want to take specific clothes along for after the competition, list them and pack them. If you want specific music for the ride there and during warm-ups, list it and pack it. If you have a certain ball

When All Eyes Are On You (above). It can be overwhelming to have the eyes of coaches, teammates, opposing players, and thousands of fans all directed at you. Practice getting comfortable with being on stage and executing while being watched. Narrow your focus to what's important: your strengths, your swing, and your confidence. What crowd?

The PRE Competition Routines (above) are purposeful mental activities to prepare for the confidence battle. Practice crashing and recovering a few minutes every day; it will pay big rewards when the heat is on and it's time to step up and deliver.

marker, repair tool, etc., make sure it's listed and checked off in your bag. Whatever is important to you, list it, check it, and pack it. Does this seem unnecessary? Do it anyway. The mental benefit of having a comfortable routine is what we're after.

This may seem trivial, but it's not. For the big shows you need to make yourself as psychologically comfortable as possible and your *things* help accomplish that.

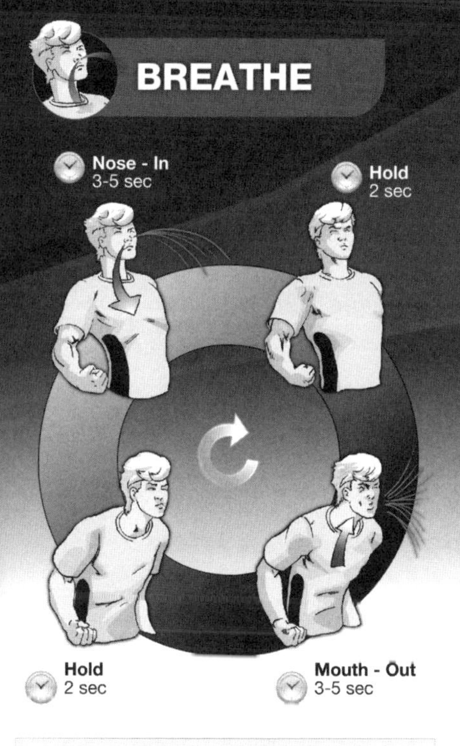

Why put out the extra effort to make a list? When there are a lot of items to organize and you don't want to leave anything behind, a list provides assurance. When you're not thinking about what you might have forgotten to pack, you're then able to think about the stuff that matters, like rehearsing Doubt Demon counterattacks.

Little Dogs: Your mother is not your list. Do it yourself.

Don't pack your bags until you've gathered everything in a group on the floor in front of you and can check it off as you pack. Plan and be organized and meticulous about packing your competition necessities. Not only will you have everything you want and need at the competition, but your mind will be in a calm and focused place—a narrow competition mindset.

#2 Fuel:

Nutrition is undervalued by practically everyone. But if your goal is to be a consistent pressure-ready competitor, especially at the big tournaments, *nutrition cannot be ignored.*

To compete on a superior level, our bodies need clean-burning, high-octane, quick-recovery fuel: fresh fruits, grains, nuts, and good fats—not weak, low-energy food imposters like candy, burgers, hot dogs, chips, plastic cheese, and colored sugar-water, just to name a few.

Nutrition is so important that I've devoted an entire chapter to it. Chapter 3 will help you think of food more functionally than emotionally. It shows you how to *fuel* for Big Dog performances rather than just eating to please your taste buds.

You'll find out why fats are the most important fuel for your competitive fire, and why any kind of refined sugar can be devastating to your high-performance competitive machine.

Consider the following: The brain makes up 2% of a person's bodyweight but consumes 20% of the available energy—even while resting. Additionally, our brain and its amazing neurons, unlike muscle, cannot store extra energy—it's completely dependent on a continuous new supply from the bloodstream. Now consider an intense, five-hour, highly competitive round of golf. If you don't know how to fuel, by the time you get to the finishing holes you'll be out of gas, diminishing crisp decisions and excellent shot-making.

If you're a junk-food eater or a colored-sugar-water drinker, study Chapter 3 with heightened interest. The fueling and hydration routines are directly linked to ensuring your competitive advantage.

#3 Rest:

During competitions, resting is more for your mind than it is for your body. The mental strain of maintaining emotional stability over the span of a season or the final holes of a big tournament is very draining and requires frequent mental regrouping.

During a round, figuring out how to take mental breaks between shots is vital to stringing one well-thought-out and well-executed shot after the next. Think about it—how many other activities in your life require intense concentration for four or five hours straight? Typically none. Expecting your brain to function at a high level without conditioning it first is like trying to do a 360 your first time on a snowboard. It's not gonna happen. Being able to concentrate requires training and rest.

For me, briefly closing my eyes and controlling my breathing for only ten to fifteen seconds is incredibly refreshing during a competitive round. If doing something like that makes you feel too self-conscious, get creative choosing when, where, and how to rest. I have no problem turning away from the action on the tee box or the green, leaning on a club and disconnecting for a few seconds, especially if I just executed well. I want to savor that shot—positive feeds positive.

If being in the tee box or around the green feels too exposed for you, fairways offer many opportunities to breathe and rest for a few seconds. I figured out how to close my eyes about 70% and breathe as I walk up the fairway. Another opportunity to regroup mentally is when fellow competitors prepare for their second shots; it's a perfect time to disconnect and rest a bit.

During any significant slowdown in the pace of play or definitely when making the turn, fuel, hydrate, breathe, close your eyes, and chill. Don't be concerned with that weird feeling when you open your eyes and reconnect—that's a good thing. Within a split second, you'll be refocused with renewed energy.

For optimal course management and crisp execution, do your best to figure out how to rest on each hole or at least several times during a round. In other words, construct a rest routine.

Language note: If "rest" seems too much like going to bed or taking a nap, and it doesn't make sense how to rest and compete at the same time, give the routine a different name: regroup, power-up, refocus, whatever works—just make sure you do it.

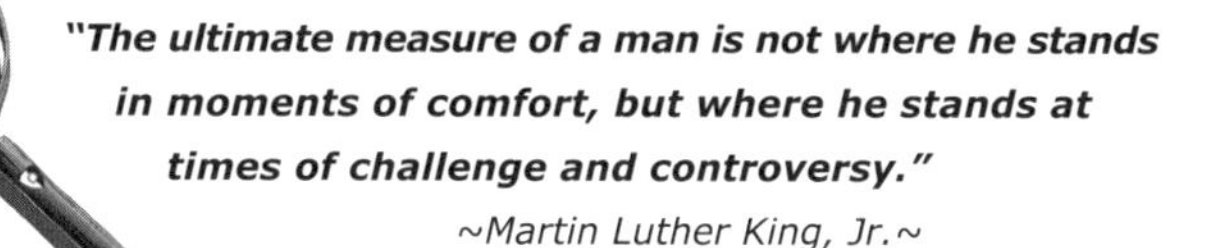

#4 Breathe:

Oxygen, along with the controlled physical inhale/exhale process, has such a positive, measured effect on emotional stability under pressure that I've made it a formal routine.

In Chapter 5, I explain deep, rhythmic breathing in detail. It's a key part of the LIVE competition skills as well. Deep, rhythmic breathing will probably become one of your favorite and most commonly used Let's Win! routines.

#5 Rehearse:

You know by now that clutch performances are not tied to genetics or luck; they're tied to the mental toughness skills that produce emotional control. Rehearsing is another way of making your mind do what you want it to do, when you want it to do it. Even when your emotional brain is freaking out, you are still in control. Choosing what your mind thinks about is the *master skill* required for high-level performances.

Realize that you can mentally rehearse anyplace where external concentration is not required: when you're on the bus, riding in the car, or lying in bed at night. What are you rehearsing? Strategies to defend against Doubt Demon attacks and emotional meltdowns. Yes, strategies. Auto-response strategies actually. Chapters 5 and 6 will delve much deeper into the mental rehearsal skills and routines for both before and during competitions.

In summary, the PRE Competition Skills and Routines are specific mental activities that enable you to consistently stay emotionally balanced and focused when it's all on the line.

Now let's move on to the Battle Zones technique.

The Battle Zones

One of the broad goals of the Let's Win! *narrowing* skill is to turn the unfamiliar into the familiar, the uncomfortable into the comfortable, so you can have more fun competing, and ultimately win.

The Battle Zones familiarity technique assists the narrowing process. It helps you mentally deal with the *unfamiliar* aspects at any course by comparing the *familiar* aspects of every course. All courses are similar in one way or another, so every competition can be mentally controlled from four familiar locations: the driving range, the tee box, the fairway, and the green.

CONQUER DISTRACTION

Nothing exists outside the Battle Zones, absolutely nothing.

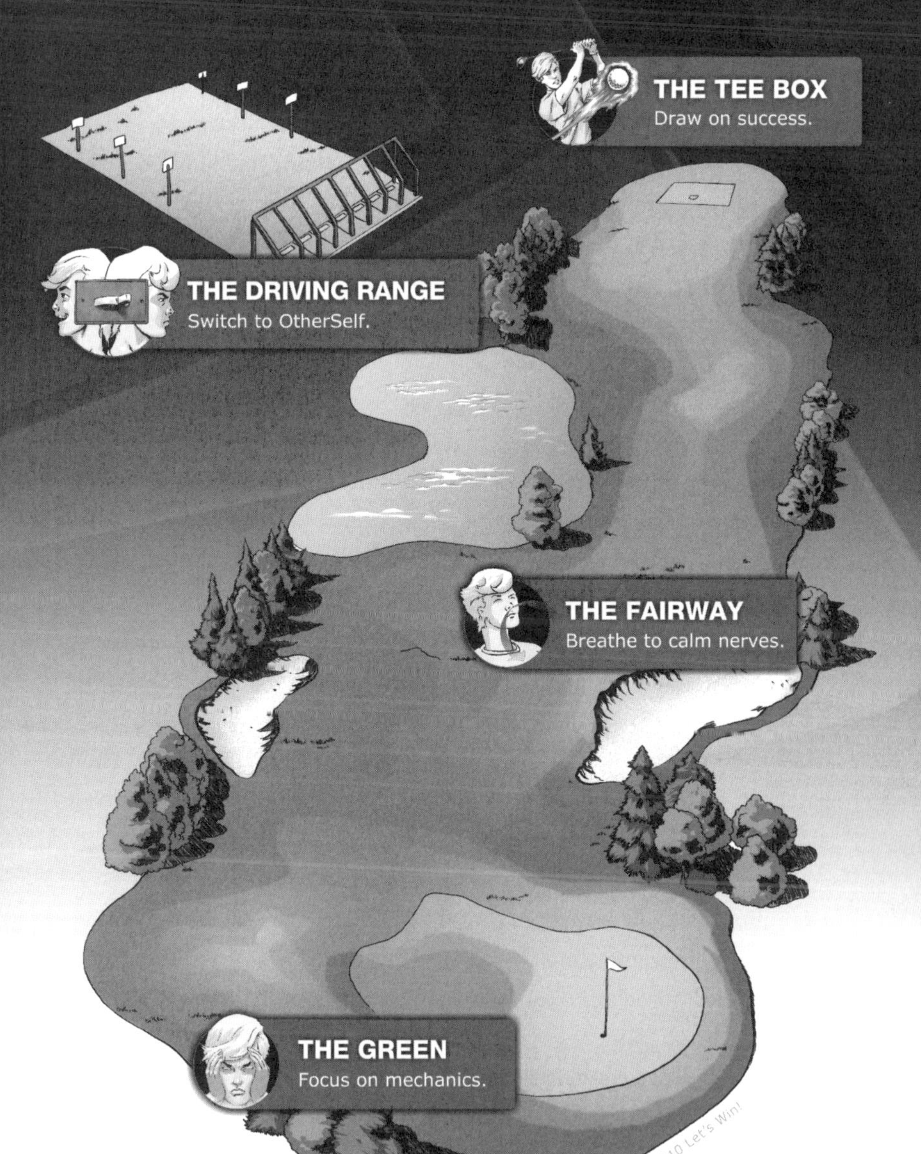

The Battle Zones (above) are four familiar locations on every course. Mentally reduce all golf courses to just those four locations; it's easier to focus on what's important rather than allowing the surroundings and all of the commotion to confuse and distract you.

Why is isolating these four locations important? So you can easily focus under a doubt attack. Think of a competition as if you're walking across a narrow beam high off the ground. What's the first rule? Don't look down. Why? Because looking down will break your concentration by engaging your fear, causing you to lose your center of balance, stumble, and literally make yourself fall. The golf course presents the same kind of mental challenge. Engaging the chaos that is always going on somewhere puts you inside the chaos and the chaos inside of you.

Being uncomfortable with a particular course's slope or layout is playing right into the Doubt Demons' plans. They use environmental factors and distractions to attack your confidence. And since your mind can only do one thing at a time, you're either mentally distracted, dwelling on negativity, or mentally focused, believing in your abilities and skills.

Picture one of the courses where your state tournament is held, in detail. See the clubhouse, the practice green, the 1st and 10th tees, the 9th and 18th greens, the driving range, and the huge scoreboard.

As you're picturing the clubhouse and its surrounding features, also picture the whole track as a unit or theme. What is the slope? Varied, flat, twisting? Are there lots of bunkers, water hazards, wetlands, trees? Lots of uneven lies? See that course and its variations as a unit.

Got the picture? It's sort of an aerial view of a course layout. Many courses have them printed on their score cards. Viewing courses globally and comparing similarities eases tension during pressure moments.

Actually walking a new course prior to a practice round will give you a definite edge; you're giving your mind something to do that's positive. Then when it's game time, you'll have an easier time narrowing your concentration to each hole's shot requirements, your swing keys, and your confidence triggers.

Now let's take a closer look at each Battle Zone.

The Driving Range:

The first Battle Zone for many sports, where final mental preparation takes place, is the locker room. But in golf many players get out of the car or off the bus, put on their shoes, and head straight to the range or practice green. So in golf the driving range is the first Battle Zone. It's

Photo: Aaron Munson of the University of Indianapolis concentrates on lining up a putt during the Division II Men's Golf Championship held at the Loomis Trail Golf Club in Blaine, WA. *Jamie Schwaberow/ NCAA Photos*

where the emotional conflict between our Little Dog and our Big Dog, our doubtful self and our confident self, intensifies.

The range is not only a place to warm up your body and groove your swing—more importantly it's also a place to kick in some LBi and engage your competition mindset. Monkey Mode is constantly lurking and on the range there's still time to quiet the nerves and center yourself. Breathe and concentrate on why you can, instead of why you can't.

Chapter 6 provides much greater detail on how to best utilize the range to boost your confidence before stepping onto the first tee. For now, understand that the driving range is where you transition from friendly to competitive, where you integrate your left brain, *switch* to your competitive OtherSelf, and get serious.

The Tee Box:

The last range ball has been hit. You make your way through the hundred or so spectators surrounding the first tee. The announcer calls your name and your heart jumps. You cinch your glove, jam your tee into the box and place the ball just the way you like it. The club feels weird in your hands. Your mind is racing. Your eyes dart everywhere. You can barely feel your feet on the ground. You take a couple of practice swings, try to swallow, but your mouth is bone dry. At that moment many competitors would rather drop to their knees and make a pact with some universe super force instead of take the heat directly, "Please, just let me hit the fairway and I'll do anything!" Spotlights are intense.

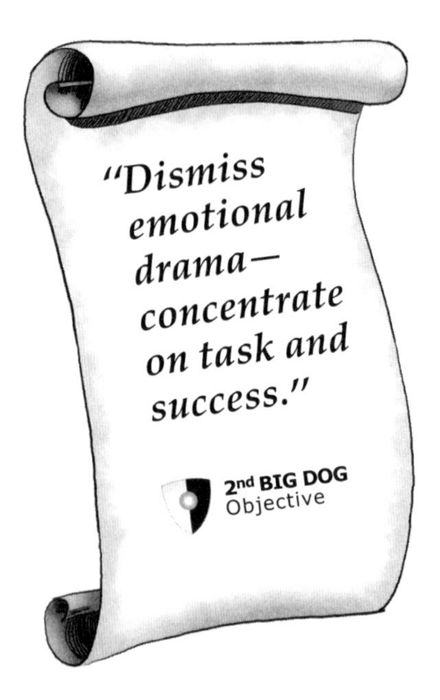

If you're naturally more timid than bold, every shot can be like the above description—one intensely negative, desperate moment after the next.

The key to handling the heat on the tee box is preparing for those intense, uncomfortable feelings of being isolated and looked at. Those few seconds right before making contact are a highly-aware mental space. We just need to get out of our own way and *do it.* We're focused directly on the ball in front of us, but simultaneously we have a physical sense of all of the space around us and everyone who's watching. It's a physical-mental-emotional experience very similar to giving a presentation in front of a group. We acutely see ourselves doing what we're doing, which can be very unnerving. Then, bring the Doubt Demons into the picture and it can be complete mental chaos.

Rehearse feeling those feelings of being looked at, because every tee shot produces the same awareness, and always will, unless you're on the range or playing by yourself.

Try rehearsing with a fantasy crowd. Run vivid mental simulations of being at the center of attention; get accustomed to the all-eyes-on-you sensation. After repeated mental practice, you'll notice how much less chaotic center-stage emotions will become.

Work toward being able to be aware of being looked at while stepping up to the ball and confidently thinking to yourself, *"Yeah, everyone's staring at me, so, bring it on!"*

The Fairway:

Keep in mind that the primary purpose of the Battle Zone familiarizing technique is to predictably increase your emotional comfort level on any course in the country. To prepare you to be comfortable wherever you go, so there's minimal mystery or drama.

Just like a tee box is a tee box, a fairway is a fairway. Yeah, the layout, slope, grass, and hazards are all different, some more difficult than others, but fairways are fundamentally the same. The features that make each fairway unique are also the things that they all have in common. Of course we need to make some minor mental adjustments the first time we play a new course, but once we purposefully compare similarities and distance relationships between that course and our favorite course, and then adjust our thinking, presto, we're *home*.

We do this comparing activity somewhat automatically, "Oh, this is just like ...." We're mentally picturing something familiar. With this technique, just be a little more mentally active and detailed; compare the similarities and the differences. This process helps each course feel more familiar, which will put you more at ease.

The greater familiarity you have with your surroundings, the easier it is to narrow your focus and believe in *why* you can execute the shot. If you can answer the *why* question with conviction, what is there to be nervous about? You've done it before, so do it again.

But, in order to do *you must believe,* and your conviction will constantly be tested. You see yourself executing like a Big Dog, but then BAM! the next vision you see is yourself hesitating and messing up. Maintaining crisp focus under pressure is a violent emotional roller coaster and to ride it successfully requires as much familiarity as possible.

Concentrate on what is directly in front of you, which is familiar, rather than what is *out there* on the course, which is unfamiliar. Convince your mind that you know that fairway and the shot required. Compare it to the many similar shots you've made before on other fairways.

If you practice this mental technique, there is absolutely no reason to be uncomfortable on a new course, because every course is home—mentally you own it.

The Green:

While every shot is just as important as the other, must-make putts are in a class by themselves in terms of pressure. The green is where we seriously battle our doubtful selves, because we have the highest expectations of ourselves, "I should have made that putt!"

The rules of the game give the player the stage for every shot, which is so cool, but being on the green is a different all-eyes-on-you pressure experience. It's where you must seriously claim territory. Life slows to just you and the putt, which is a problem if you don't know how to focus your thinking. We have way too much time to think the wrong things. The green is where the Doubt Demons take advantage of numerous doubt triggers. It truly is a confidence battle zone.

This is why pre-shot routines are so effective; they force our minds to think about the things that make putts, like line and pace, rather than thinking about all the ways to miss putts.

Typically, as we step off a putt and circle the hole trying to figure out the break and the pace, we're also listening to a serious internal battle between our Little Dog and our Big Dog. Unfortunately, our Little Dog often times makes more noise, which is what these mental toughness skills are going to change. Along with figuring out the physics of a putt, you also need to be telling yourself *why* you can make that putt. Learn to listen to your Big Dog competitive self.

To make more putts, narrow your focus to just line, pace, and your personal putting stroke keys. Summon some emotional intelligence and let your Big Dog out. You believing in you is the only believing that counts.

Mentally reducing all golf courses to four Battle Zones will help you deal with your surroundings more positively, rather than allowing your surroundings to confuse and distract you.

Staying Focused

Conquering tournament distractions requires focus; there's just no way around it. Staying focused requires a competition mindset and that mindset boils down to a simple perspective: *It's not social.*

When competing, the everyday demands of life must be put on hold: social demands, work demands, and all other goal demands. Nothing matters except the next shot—absolutely nothing. You have to be *emotionally selfish* before and during competitions to maintain a competitively focused frame of mind. Everything else is pure distraction.

Use the Let's Win! narrow technique to concentrate on your game plan and execution. A little watching the competition isn't bad while you're waiting for your turn, but don't get emotionally involved. The less you engage what is going on around you, the more focused you'll be on what you need to do to execute the next great shot. Mentally focus on controlling your competitive emotions and remember that all of life's other demands can wait until you're through competing for the day.

Travel

If you've made it to a title tournament (districts, regionals, or state), you are obviously doing a lot of things right. The primary concerns then, more than ever, are avoiding distractions and staying emotionally balanced.

Warning: Just because you've made it to a big show does not mean it's time to celebrate. That's a bad move. I've seen it happen too many times, athletes running all around, whooping and hollering, just getting off focus. Don't release all of that pent-up emotional energy—it's your power.

Here's the situation: You've been committed for months and have competed well enough to make it out of your league and it feels great. A couple of more rounds and it could be the ultimate celebration. A couple of more rounds and you could be holding a championship trophy high over your head. Getting to the big time is a tremendous accomplishment and naturally you feel like celebrating. But wait! Get a grip—seriously.

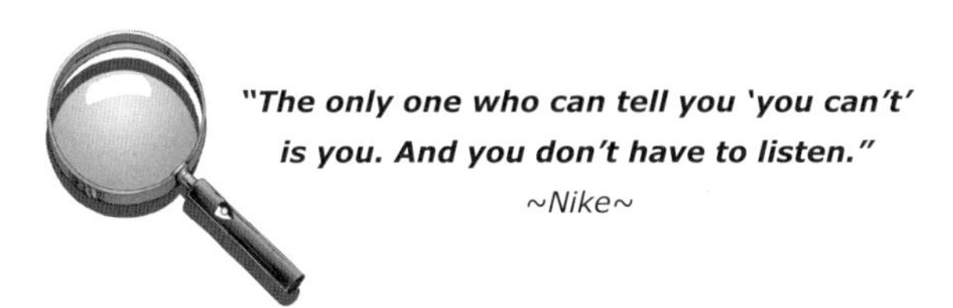

Narrow your focus and concentrate on execution and your confidence—dismiss emotional drama.

Oops ... first I should ask about your dream. Is your dream to be a champion or a participant? If it's just to participate at districts or state, go celebrate. If it's to win the championship, put your head down and focus.

Big tournament distractions can be severe. Your emotions are on overload because you actually have a shot at the dream. The next few rounds may be the most important of your competitive life. For many of you, your mind and emotions are everywhere. The central focus is to keep doing what you've been doing. Whatever you've been doing mentally to get there, keep doing it. It's okay to accept congratulations from Grandpa and Grandma, but keep your emotions in check. Humbly accept the congratulations, but stay serious inside—keep that *narrow* competition mindset. There is still a lot of work to do.

One of the key problems with maintaining focus before and during the big shows is dealing with your own pent-up emotions, your teammates' pent-up emotions, your coaches' pent-up emotions, and all your peers' bright, smiling, congratulatory faces. Everyone means well, but mostly it's pure distraction. Yeah, all of the attention is great, but it's nothing but distraction. Keep your competition mindset fully engaged. That competitive OtherSelf you've created is who needs to be in charge, not your social self. I'm not suggesting intensely focusing all of the time, I'm just saying don't emotionally celebrate. I'm suggesting keeping your mind where it needs to be, which is focused on competing, not socializing and celebrating. Save that for after finals. Then it's time to party!

The discipline required at a travel tournament is probably the hardest discipline to master—especially for teens. Not only do you want to run around and make the most of your adventure, you also want to constantly socialize. Go ahead, if your ultimate goal is not to win.

Here comes the dad/coach, stern-faced, finger-pointing speech: Get a grip! Why are you there? Why have you worked so hard? Make positive, disciplined decisions that will propel you toward victory, as opposed to leaving you sitting in dejection. Stay focused and concentrate on what's important, which is competing, not socializing and fooling around. Don't blow it once you get to state or an important title tournament. Plotting and indulging in social activities diverts your focus and lowers your competitive intensity. Like it or not, winning a state tournament takes an extraordinary level of concentration and conviction; it isn't supposed to be a full-on social adventure. So concentrate on doing your very best; it's all up to you, no one can force you to focus.

This travel point is important, so let's look at it from a different angle. For many of you, traveling with your team is a new experience and emotionally you treat it like some sort of vacation. I've seen the distractions at state and nationals derail many would-be champions because they lost their competitive focus and decided (unconsciously) to indulge themselves socially. I encourage you to keep your head on straight, discipline yourself, and conserve your energy for the tournament. In other words, when you're off the course, don't deviate from your competition mindset. I'm not suggesting sitting in the corner of the hotel room in a yoga position with a towel over your head, but if your focus wanders before the tournament, it's likely that you will suffer some sort of negative consequences.

This isn't a karma thing; it's a concentration thing. The mind can only do one thing at a time. *Switching* from a friendly mindset to competition mindset isn't easy for most of us. While we do turn off our laser-beam concentration a lot of the time, during the post season we must keep at least one eye on the prize 24/7. Mentally wandering—fully engaging in social activities—is a big mistake.

Trust me, tournaments are not the place to play social games. Enjoy your teammates and other competitors from out of town, but the mind and habits of a confident Big Dog competitor are focused and determined. Try not to fall into the trap of mistaking an away tournament as some sort of fun outing or vacation—it's not Disneyland. It's a competition. At tournaments you need to be the most patient, the most focused, and the most disciplined. Yeah, have fun, but don't forget why you're there—you're there to compete, and win.

The Unexpected

Another key element to maintaining emotional stability, keeping the Doubt Demons at arm's length, is learning how to deal with the unexpected. Gear issues can be a little unnerving even for a seasoned competitor. Leaving a piece of gear behind, losing it, or having a piece of gear break can be very distracting.

So what do you do if you leave a special piece of gear behind, lose it, or it breaks? First, don't react like a rookie; it's not that critical—don't come unglued. Yes, it's your favorite, it feels the best, and you're the most comfortable with it. So… it's only gear. Shift gears (no pun intended) and make the necessary mental adjustments. Don't allow it to become a distraction. In other words, do what you must do to compete, adapt and overcome. A gladiator would pick up *any* weapon in the Colosseum—would you?

No matter what goes wrong, because undoubtedly things *will* go wrong, remain composed. Caring about anything that gets in your way, including gear issues, is poorly-directed mental/emotional energy. Big Dog competitors *adapt and overcome,* no matter the situation.

Practice, Practice, Practice

Just like consistently practicing various golf shots so you can use them with confidence under pressure, mental toughness skills and the ability to narrow our concentration require similar amounts of attention. Not so much in time spent, but rather in gaining a quality of understanding. But no matter how you look at it, it's the same old story: practice, practice, practice.

At first, practice is nothing more than trying to understand the idea. The next step is using the skills and techniques in an actual practice. Then, after numerous practice sessions, it's showtime.

The more you practice mentally preparing, the more these concepts become actual skills. Skills you can rely on in the heat of the moment.

The underlying point throughout this chapter is you can conquer course commotion and dismiss emotional drama by equipping yourself with the mental skills needed to *narrow your focus* to what's important: the mechanics of the current shot, your personal swing keys, and your confidence triggers.

The PRE Competition Routines and the Battle Zones familiarity technique prepare you mentally for the emotional drama and doubtful thinking that will always accompany pressure situations—always. So *narrow* your concentration and focus on your strengths—let your Big Dog out!

CHAPTER 2

REVIEW

Narrow: Conquer Course Chaos

Summary

Competitive environments are threatening and confusing, sometimes overwhelming, and regularly full of distractions. *Narrowing* our focus to shot requirements, swing keys, and positive triggers is what effectively blocks out distractions and reduces emotional chaos, allowing us to concentrate more intently on what's important: *our confidence.*

Test—What did you learn?

True/False Statements:

1) We block out distractions by narrowing our focus to some thing positive.
2) Narrowing our concentration helps reduce emotional chaos.
3) Making it to a title tournament means it's time to celebrate.
4) Periodically resting the mind is essential to maintaining concentration over long hours.

Do It!

Identify places in your life when you narrow your focus, when you consciously choose what you're thinking about. Then, repeat the narrowing process in emotionally challenging situations. Don't let the Doubt Demons get the best of you. Practice narrowing in everyday life, so you can focus and concentrate more easily in the heat of the moment.

CHAPTER 3

FUEL

Power Your Performance

In this chapter you will learn how to *fuel*—mental toughness skill #3—a competition skill that changes our eating habits from taste preferences to nutrient preferences for faster recovery and rock solid performances.

Our Big Dog self
prefers to *fuel* for high-powered
performances, rather than just eat for
taste and convenience.

ssential. Crucial. Vital. Do I have your attention? Nutrition is extremely important. Other than controlling doubt (by integrating your left brain), I don't know of any other aspect of high-level competition that has greater significance.

Focused concentration, excellent decision making, and crisp execution throughout an entire season are what it takes to make the postseason. One missed clutch shot can alter future opportunities. Why risk a mental error because you were out of gas? Having quick, new energy for immediate mental recovery is essential. Think of food as fuel, not a pleasure item.

Food Is Fuel

Think of food more functionally (what you need) than emotionally (what you want), especially for tournaments. Food is fuel, so *control your tongue*. Think about what your mind and body need to recover and be ready for the next shot, rather than what tastes good. For outstanding performances, choose high-octane, quick-recovery, Big Dog fuel over weak, low-energy tongue food.

Here's a simple test. You're on your way to practice and forgot to eat earlier. You have the option to quickly breeze through a fast food drive-thru, or to park and go inside a grocery store for some healthy items. Which do you choose? If you're inclined to do the first choice, either because the food is tastier or quicker, then you definitely need to pay attention to this chapter. Eating properly sometimes takes more effort—but then doesn't everything that produces a benefit?

You don't have to become a nutritionist in order to understand the basic differences between fueling for performance as opposed to eating for taste. Stay with me here and I'll keep this as simple as possible.

The Food Court (above) vividly illustrates the choices you have several times each day, every day. Do you eat toxic junk that has been modified to taste good or consume nature's fuel for optimal focus, crisp decisions, and solid execution? The choice is yours. Choose wisely.

Think of food as types and sources. Types: proteins, carbs, and fats. Sources: natural or processed. Blending carbs and fats from natural sources results in high-octane, quick-recovery, Big Dog fuel.

Proteins

On tournament day, proteins are not premium energy sources, because proteins are like wet logs on a fire—they don't burn quickly. The body uses proteins to rebuild muscle and other cells; it doesn't easily use proteins as

gasoline (energy). Before and during a round is not the time to rebuild cells. Before and during a round is the time to fill your empty gas tank.

Protein is a good thing at night, when you're through practicing or competing for the day. In fact, when not competing you need protein throughout the day for a variety of reasons.

The primary sources of non-vegetarian protein are beef, poultry, and fish. Tuna is a great source of protein and other important nutrients (e.g., omega fats). Processed junk foods like burgers, fries, shakes, or soda pop, have very little of what your body needs to compete, which is pure energy. Processed junk food is the last thing your body needs before, during, or after a demanding practice or intense tournament.

You probably haven't thought about it much, so don't think I'm doggin' you. I'm just criticizing poor, mindless, low-energy, tongue-related choices, in the context of competitive athletics.

The *Foodcourt* illustration on the previous page offers a great example of premium sources from nature vs. processed, toxic junk. Do your best, at least during the season and definitely before and during tournaments, to eat from premium, natural, high-energy sources. You'll feel the difference almost instantly. I'll provide more on premium, natural sources later in this chapter.

Carbs & Fats

Carbs and fats are the kindling for your internal fire. They are the *types* of food that provide immediately usable energy. Effectively combining carbs and fats is the key to having a *full* gas tank that can sustain intense concentration.

Remember, our brain consumes 20% of our total available energy and it does not have the capacity to store energy, so it relies on a constant new supply from the bloodstream.

Think of carbs and fats like the paper, twigs, and dry logs you would use to build a fire. The paper and twigs are carbs—thin, quick fuel. Fats are the dry logs—denser, longer burning fuel. Proteins are like wet, green wood that just lie there smoldering.

Picture being on a camping trip with your friends and it's time to start a camp fire. Are you going to start by trying to light wet, green wood with a match? Don't think so. You'll start with ultra-dry kindling that will ignite easily—paper and dry twigs. Get the point?

Split carbs into two categories: simple (paper) and complex (twigs). As competitors wanting to excel, we need a small amount of simple and a large amount of complex. Fruit is a simple carb (paper), and the quickest energy to get into the blood stream. The body doesn't have to do much to natural fruit sugar to burn it instantly.

Natural whole grains are complex carbs (twigs). The body has to work a little harder to digest whole grains, but they provide a longer burning energy stream, unlike fruit (paper), which is *poof*—gone.

Fats are probably the least understood, but the most important *fuel* for your competitive fire. Your body loves fat because it's concentrated, dense energy. There is twice as much energy (calories) in one gram of fat than there is in one gram of carbohydrate. Fats are the real dry logs for your body's furnace.

Photo: A great shoulder turn on the tee at the Mountain West Conference Men's Golf Championship at Tucson National's Catalina Course, in Tucson, Arizona. *Trevor Brown, Jr./NCAA Photos*

Some of the misinformation you may have read includes the idea that fat slows digestion. That's incorrect. The right way to look at fat is that it's *slower to digest*. Since fat has twice the energy it burns slower than carbs, which is a good thing.

Example: Think of trying to keep a fire blazing for hours. If you just use paper and twigs, you can't do it. The fire will blaze for about ten minutes and then die out. Not even a coal will be left. Similarly, if you try and run on just carbs, you'll run out of fuel midway through the round—when you need it most—so you'll need to work some fats into your fuel plan. Are you getting this fuel/fire/competition energy metaphor? Think of food as fuel, not a pleasure item.

Sugars

Sugars are part of the carb family, and refined sugars are everywhere. They can be so devastating to competitive concentration and physical timing that they deserve closer attention.

Sugary foods and drinks like pop, honey, corn syrup (a sugar additive), and fructose (another sugar additive), have absolutely no place in a focused, Big Dog competitor's diet—at all, ever!

Be sure to read your food's labels carefully. If you were a competitive motocross rider, you would know exactly what type of fuel you were putting in your bike, along with a host of other high-performance-related issues. See the comparison?

Sugary foods that are processed for *better flavor* get pretty beat up during the processing. Their cell walls become weak and easy to breakdown. Due to the processing, the energy enters the bloodstream too quickly, almost as if injected by a syringe. I call this sugar dumping—a common eating habit that can be tied directly to poor decision making and sloppy execution.

When we eat sugary foods, our blood sugar (glucose) elevates instantly, but rises too far above the optimal level. When this happens, our bodies tell the pancreas to secrete insulin, which causes cells throughout our body to pull the extra sugar out of the bloodstream to store it. Guess what happens next. Yep, we crash. The insulin effect robs the available energy from our bloodstreams leaving us quickly depleted. Hence, we make poor decisions and display hesitant execution.

The deeper understanding here, as we discussed, is that our brain cannot store extra energy—it is totally dependent on a continuous new supply from the bloodstream. When we dump sugar, soon after the

Fuel—mental skill #3 (above). Blend carbs and fats from premium sources; it results in high-octane, quick-recovery fuel. Remember, our Little Dog self eats for pleasure, while our Big Dog self fuels for optimal performances.

insulin effect takes hold, the brain goes into crisis mode. We feel weak, confused, spaced-out, nervous and indecisive, and there are many other negative side effects. And it's all because of a taste-driven sugar craving. Get off the sugar rollercoaster.

The key to building a great fire—having a *full* gas tank—is combining unprocessed carbs and fats, giving us short- and long-term energy. Get rid of refined, processed sugar.

Review the high-octane *Fuel Groups* examples on the previous page, and limit yourself to those or similar choices. Think with your Big Dog competition mindset, not with your Little Dog tongue—if not every day, then at least throughout the season and especially before and during tournaments. Make intelligent fuel choices for championship performances rather than sugar-driven pleasure preferences.

Premium Natural Sources

Premium sources of food and fluids come from nature. They haven't been processed or modified from their original states. This is a pretty simple concept to understand. If food has gone through a machine—had anything taken from it or added to it—it's been processed. Processed food is tongue food, not mind-and-body food. Nature provides premium fuel for sustained energy. Machines do not.

The majority of the time, man-made products like protein bars have been altered; preservatives have been added for longer shelf life and flavor enhancers have been added for better taste. This processing alters the structure of the food and makes it harder for your body to burn efficiently. The additives are an additional issue, but I won't go into how unhealthy processed foods are, I'll just stay focused on their burning capability.

A positive note is that healthy snacks are on the rise. Some "bar" companies are making their products with organic (not processed), pure ingredients, so if you like the convenience of bars, do a little research and look at the ingredients list. Choose a brand which uses only natural ingredients: oats, fruit, peanut butter, etc. If you can't pronounce an ingredient, typically it's not natural. If you have to consume a packaged product, buy one that is both a great fuel source and good for you.

Another problem with most bars is that they're very low in calories and extremely low in fat. Typically, most bars are around 200–230 calories with less than five grams of fat. For most of you, that means about twenty minutes worth of medium-grade fuel, even if you choose a bar from premium sources. So, if you eat a bar on the turn with the idea that you're completely fueling up, you're not; by the 14th hole you'll be out of gas, especially if you're emotionally activated. A wholegrain bagel and cream cheese, a wholegrain peanut butter and jelly sandwich, or a nut mix are much better choices than just a bar. You need ample fuel, *not taste and convenience.*

The *Foodcourt* back on page 50 offers a humorous, exaggerated view of the premium fuel vs. toxic junk debate. One side represents premium sources from nature while the other side represents processed, toxic junk: burgers, fries, shakes, hot dogs, soda pop, chips and plastic cheese, and processed pizza from concession stands are not premium Big Dog fuel sources.

Disclaimer: Realize that burgers, fries, shakes, and pizza are not villains in and of themselves, it's the source the ingredients come from that matters. A burger made from lean organic beef, a wholegrain bun, fresh organic vegetables, and organic condiments is awesome. The same goes for pizza: wholegrain dough, organic sauce, free range meats, real cheese, fresh veggies, etc. Fries are great, if they're real potatoes fried in real, premium oil. A shake is awesome, if it's from whole milk, real ice cream, fresh organic berries, minus the added sugar syrup. Got the picture? It's about the source, not about the *type* of food.

I hope this information is getting inside that taste-driven head and you're starting to see the difference between Big Dog tournament fuel and Little Dog processed tongue food.

You can eat poisonous, toxic junk all year long if you need to—yuck! But I encourage you to consume mostly high-octane Big Dog fuel during the season. Look past your taste preferences and think about what your mind and body need to recover from the extreme energy drain of long practices and intense competitions.

Food is fuel, so the choice is either powerful or weak.

Tournament Fueling

The first type of food to eat a couple of hours before a round should be a real piece of fruit: banana, orange, or apple. Consume a simple carb (paper) first, which will immediately put fuel in your tank; it will quickly increase your blood sugar level, and you'll feel fueled instantly. Wash it down with water.

After the initial piece of fruit and water comes a carb/fat combo: a wholegrain bagel and cream cheese, or a wholegrain bagel and peanut butter, or a wholegrain peanut butter and jelly, plus a nut mix on the side. Stay away from meat (protein).

The amount of carb/fat combo you need depends on your size. If you're less than 125 pounds you may only need one serving, but if you're 150 pounds plus, you may need a couple, but don't overdo it. Nerves are sparking the morning of a tournament, so control yourself, don't make yourself uncomfortable. Take a break and let your digestive system go to work. After twenty minutes or so if you're still not full, go back for more, but the second time *skip the fruit*. Grab another carb/fat combo. Once you're full, there's probably at least one hour or so before starting warm-ups, so put on your headphones, breathe, kick in some LBi mental toughness to lessen the nerves, and let your body absorb the calories.

Take premium snacks and water with you as you head out on the front. If you're well-fueled before teeing off, then you'll be fine until you get to the 7th or 8th hole, which is typically two hours into the round. Don't wait for the turn or until you feel hungry. By then your blood sugar will be down and your crispness, both physically and mentally, will be lessened. Nut/fruit mixes are great when we're competing. A couple of handfuls with some water every hour or so will sustain your blood sugar level, and you will finish strong, with a clear head. That's minus the candy of course—no sugar.

On the turn, go for a carb/fat combo, not a burger or hot dog. Even though meat may taste good and be what you typically eat, the protein is just dead weight, so focus on premium carbs and fats.

On the back, you may need to snack every couple of holes. Not a lot, just enough to stabilize your energy level, so as you attack the finishing holes, the holes that typically decide who emerges the champion, you'll have power that sustains excellent decisions and purposeful swings.

Between Rounds

At the big tournaments, when there are multiple rounds to win, continue to think fueling, not eating. It's pretty simple. Yes, you'll want some protein for dinner, but keep it light. Check out the fuel examples to the right for

FUELING SEQUENCE

Make intelligent, planned, high-performance choices.

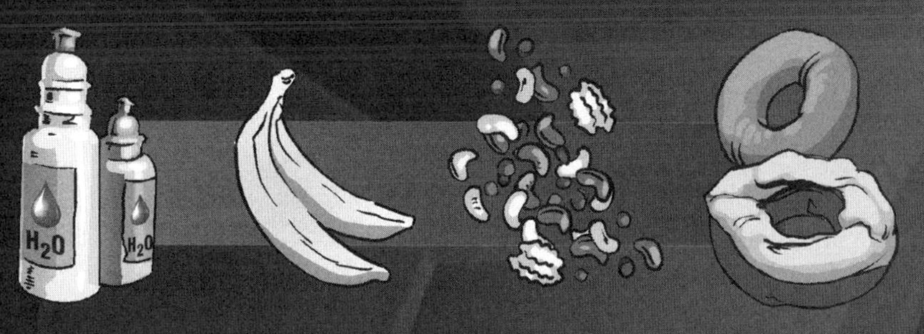

WATER + FRUIT + COMBO + COMBO

Nature's food is optimal. Combine premium sources of carbs and fats. **Hydrate** with water, not sports drinks.

Below: Protein options for multi-day tournaments and road trips.

Turkey Sandwich | **Grilled Fish/Chicken Pasta/Rice/Veggies** | **Stuffed Potato** | **Chicken Wrap**

The Fueling Sequence examples (above) provide sustained energy for before and during a competition: water, fruit, carb/fat combo. Think with less emotion and more common sense when it comes to food; in other words mute your taste buds to make wise, high-performance fuel choices.

Our Little Dog focuses on taste, while our Big Dog focuses on fuel. So our Little Dog needs to get over it.

dinner options. Also, if you played in the heat and you've sweated off a few pounds, you're going to need lots of water, not sports drinks and soda pop. I'll explain why sports drinks are not premium in the next section.

Additionally, rest is critical between rounds, so fuel up and *get horizontal* as soon as possible after finishing, at least for an hour or so to start the recuperation process for the next day. As you now know, resting is more for your mind and emotions than it is for your body.

Colored Sugar-Water

Sports drinks—wow! A lot of athletes seriously dislike this information. But I've got to give it to you, because knowledge is power, and power leads to success.

Like it or not, despite what the companies who sell colored sugar-water want you to believe, the stuff is not all that. The claim of "optimally replenishing vital electrolytes and nutrients" is a marketing ploy to sell more drinks.

Our bodies are 70% water, not 70% sports drinks. So when you've sweated off a couple pounds of water, you need to replenish it with water.

There is so much garbage in many of the "ade" drinks like dyes, refined sugars, preservatives, etc., that your body has to work at discarding the garbage in order to use the water left behind. The added refined sugar is not premium fuel, so don't buy into the claim that it will help you replenish spent energy faster. Real, unprocessed fruit sugar (already explained) will get in your bloodstream quicker and burn better.

Don't confuse a piece of fruit with drinking gallons of fruit juice. A large amount of fruit juice is not recommended; it's too acidic and will cause digestive issues. To be very clear, I'm not advocating *hydrating* with fruit juice. I'm suggesting eating a single piece of fruit, before and/or midway through the round in order to elevate your blood sugar—*hydrate with water.*

Sports-drink sales people love to talk about electrolytes. (Have you seen the movie *Idiocracy?*) Sports drinks are not the optimum way to replenish and balance depleted electrolytes. A simple multi-mineral tablet, along with lots of water will do more for replenishing electrolytes, which helps you keep from cramping.

Just Google "replenish electrolytes" and you'll see what I'm talking about. Look for sources that aren't trying to sell you something and you'll get the straight information.

Recently, I happened to surf into a women's soccer website, which offered a similar opinion about sports drinks. In fact, sayo.org added the following to this discussion: "Professional and college athletes drink water at their events, even though the water comes out of Gatorade jugs." (Notice what comes out of the Gatorade jug the next time the winning coach gets doused at the end of the game: ice and water.)

Let your Big Dog out; make time to prepare meals and snacks for high-gear performances. Only Little Dogs eat for taste.

Before and during an intense round, you should stick with water until your fluid level is back where it needs to be. One of the real dangers of colored sugar-water, the ade drinks, is you become tongue/taste addicted and won't drink water, so you fail to hydrate as much as you need to.

Example: On a hot summer day you easily can sweat off several (two to four) pounds during a round. This makes hydrating with colored sugar-water difficult; it's too syrupy (sugary), and has too much junk in it. Instinctively you'll stop hydrating after a couple of pounds of sports drink. Get the math picture? For proper hydration you would need to drink one of the monster sports drink containers, the big one, the sixty-four-ounce one (four pounds). You won't do it, so you'll get dehydrated, and by the end of the round you'll be confused and disoriented.

Hydration is about function, not pleasure. Our Little Dog self focuses on taste, while our Big Dog self focuses on fuel. So our Little Dog self needs to get over it and remove taste from the equation.

Bring It With You

I rarely see coaches/teams provide fuel for their competitors, which is a bit of a mystery to me. If I were running the show there would be ample quantities of premium fuel before rounds and on the turn: fresh fruit, wholegrain bagels and cream cheese, peanut butter and jelly sandwiches, nut mixes or something similar, and gallons of water.

If your team is not one that provides fuel, put it on your list of competition necessities and bring it with you. It's not that tough; throw a couple of premium snacks in your golf bag to have greater control over better shot making.

Don't Change A Thing

If you don't add some high-octane fuel to your diet, to let your body get used to digesting premium fuel, it's probably not a good idea to make drastic changes on tournament day.

Sometimes a digestive system that only receives junk food from its owner has a hard time with premium dense-energy foods. If you're a pop-something-in-the-toaster or sugared-cereal breakfast eater, a wholegrain bagel and cream cheese might cause some digestive problems the first couple of times. Before tournaments you want to stay as close to your standard food routine as possible; it's what your body knows.

Another example of "don't change a thing" relates to breakfast when you're out-of-town at away tournaments, especially title tournaments. Be careful about going to a restaurant for the *great* breakfast before the *big* tournament. Emotionally that sounds and feels good, but unless you've eaten the great breakfast at that particular restaurant before, it's not a good idea. Stay with what your body knows. Eating breakfast at an unfamiliar restaurant on tournament day is *high risk*. You don't know what you're going to get. Plus, just because you've made it to state, doesn't mean it's time to celebrate.

If going to a restaurant is a must, be smart about your choices. Eat with premium fuel in mind, not tongue and taste habits. Personally, I wouldn't even consider going to an unfamiliar restaurant the morning of a big tournament—*not a chance!*

As we close this chapter the key point is this, being a complete athlete is about commanding a competition mindset under pressure and that requires all of the skills, including fueling (nutrition). So think of food more functionally than emotionally, especially during the season. Think about what your mind and body need to be ready for the next shot or round, not just what tastes good.

Remember, tournament day is not the day to indulge your taste buds, save that for after the competition—a victory celebration dinner is all good.

CHAPTER 3

REVIEW

Fuel: Power Your Performance

Summary

You can't expect excellent performance results without consuming high-performance fuel. Make food choices that are based on left brain nutritional energy, not right brain emotional taste. Think beyond your tongue. Premium fuel consists of proteins, carbs, and fats from unprocessed sources, and effective hydration is done with water, not sports drinks. *Fuel.*

Test—What did you learn?

True/False Statements:

1) Premium sources of fuel come from nature and are not processed.
2) Competitors should eat lots of proteins the day of a competition.
3) Sugar (candy, soda pop, honey etc.) is a great source of carbs.
4) Competitors should avoid all fats during competition.

Do It!

Behavior change is tough; many of you walk the same path over and over, even when it's bad. Start fueling, rather than just eating—break the Little Dog junk-food cycle. Think, plan, and then do it, go to the store and find some Big Dog fuel that's easy to get ahold of. *Ignore your tongue*, so you can perform to your full potential.

CHAPTER 4

OVERRIDE

Manage Your **Primal Competitive Response**

In this chapter you will learn how to *override*—mental toughness skill #4—a competition skill that positively responds to our deep-seated primal (fear) emotions, allowing us to alter the influences of our genetics and our upbringing.

Our Big Dog self
can *override* the emotional drama
by anticipating our typical
reactions to pressure.

We have all either been *that athlete* or we have seen someone in a high-stakes competition looking like they're one lump in the throat away from losing it. It's not a comfortable sight. I have often wanted to rescue them from their own worst enemies—themselves.

When athletes are overwhelmed by severe doubt, which we call a "meltdown," they have a certain look, almost like they're in shock. Their eyes glaze over and they don't respond well to conversation. They become distant, confused, and disoriented. To their detriment, they haven't equipped themselves with the skills to override a Doubt Demon attack. They haven't developed the skills to Grr up, fight back, and replace negative, doubtful thinking.

Let's face it, as long as we play competitive golf, we're going to experience nervy moments, some more intense than others. It's my goal to teach you how to *override* and defeat the Doubt Demons in those shaky moments, because after all, striking the ball pure (under pressure) is what makes competing so much fun.

The Let's Win! override skill helps us see ourselves folding under pressure and then laugh it off because we're mentally prepared and didn't get caught off guard. Then, we can drive one down the fairway instead of spraying it into the trees.

One of the goals of this chapter is to help you step out of your comfort zone—to take risks, to choose psychological danger over safety. We have to learn to be aware and anticipate "super emotional" reactions, either before or while they're happening, in order to override them and execute.

Our super emotions are involuntary, like blinking and breathing. While there are several super emotions, we'll be concentrating on our fear and intimidation response, which is controlled by our emotional brain.

The Primal Competitive Response (PCR) (above) represent how we respond to challenges of any kind. Our PCR is influenced by our genetics and our upbringing, but can be managed and even altered when we're truthful with ourselves. You evaluate your swing, right? Then why not your PCR?

For now, ponder these questions: Are you typically passive or assertive? Where do the majority of your competitive responses fit on the Grr Meter? Can you look your competitive self directly in the eyes or do you blink and turn away?

You're not afraid of evaluating your swing, right? Then don't be afraid of evaluating how you react to confrontation and to performance pressure—Grr up and take a look.

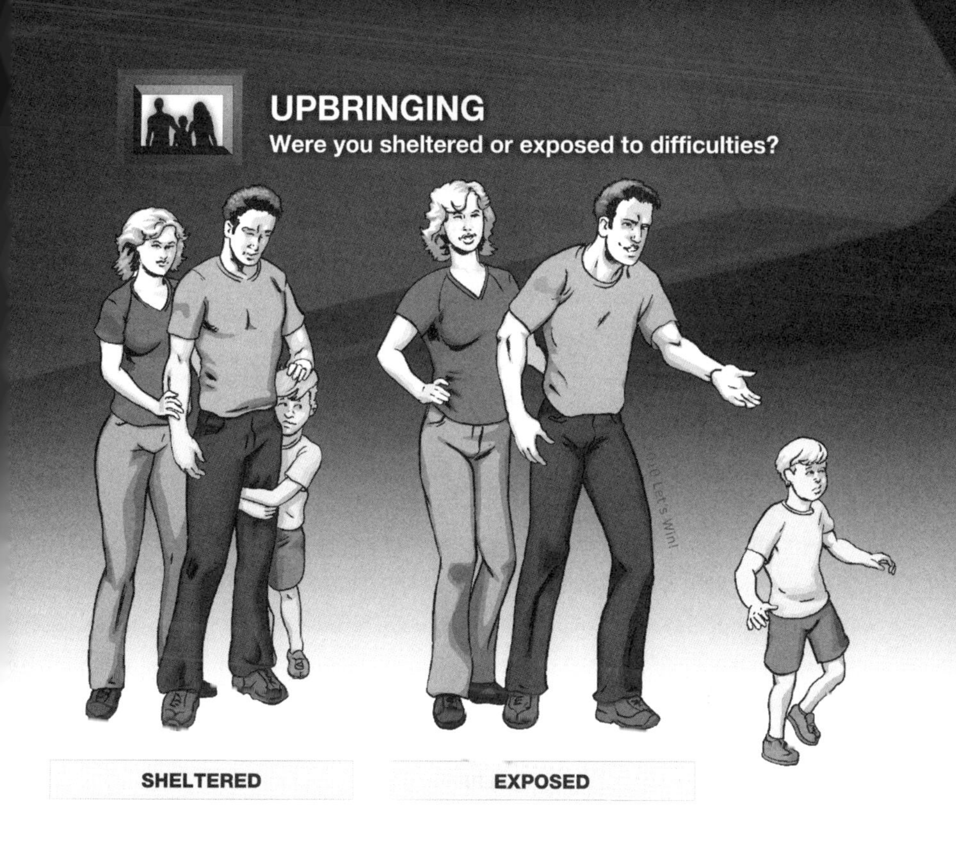

Before we probe deeper into evaluating your competitive self, let's consider how genetics and upbringing influence the way you react and behave in pressure situations. We call this typical super-emotional reaction to any kind of confrontation our "primal competitive response."

Genetics & Upbringing

I mentioned previously that even world-class competitors battle with some levels of doubt and intimidation—we all do. Additionally, we all start out at the same place, as helpless little puppies. Then, as genetics and environmental factors take over, some puppies bite and some puppies don't. The question is, "Can passive puppies learn to be assertive dogs?"

Answer: Yes they can.

Pause a minute and review the *Get Real* illustrations on the previous page, our primal competitive response. Which do you identify with? Under threat do you fight, flee, or freeze? To fight is to face confrontations straight on and to fight back against all forms of adversity; to flee is to totally avoid confrontations and to run away; to freeze is to be so petrified that you neither fight nor flee, but freeze and get run over.

Also, did (do) your parents shelter and protect you by stepping in and solving all your problems or do they encourage you to grapple with and engage the difficulties in life?

These two points are vital to understanding your typical response to competition. Genetics and upbringing do play a role, but once we understand how they both affect us, we can change or manage our typical reactions to confrontation and performance pressure.

A wolf pack is an excellent way to illustrate this point. In a pack of ten there are two Big Dog alphas, several Mid Dogs fighting for positions three through eight, and the two Little Dogs who are reduced to the scraps. Those social positions are decided as wolves mature. Usually one Big Dog male and female remain the alphas until death. However, the Mid Dogs' social positions change many times as adults. In other words, Mid Dogs don't accept being dominated and Grr up and fight back. Little Dogs struggle at the bottom their entire lives.

Realize that size does not determine a wolf's social position. It's determined by attitude and fierceness.

This wolf pack example is fitting because we humans are also social pack animals. However, what sets us apart is that we can recognize our genetics and family influences. Just because we may be small or naturally more timid does not prevent us from being fierce, confident competitors—*attitude is a choice.*

This doesn't mean we change our personalities, it simply means we manage our reactions and alter our behavior. This is one of the key concepts I'm trying to express throughout this book. Where you fit on the Dog Scale—little to big—*is up to you.*

Those who are more naturally alpha types, Big Dogs, aggressors, probably have a competitive advantage, but only while they're kids. Once the

OVERRIDE

MENTAL SKILL #4: Balance your emotional reactions.

Override—mental skill #4. No matter how our genetics and our upbringing have shaped our response to pressure, our Big Dog self can balance our emotional reactions. Override the extremes by knowing why you can believe.

more naturally timid, the Mid Dogs, see that letting their Big Dogs out is about attitude, everything changes—they learn how to show some teeth and let their Big Dogs out.

Think about it. We never earn respect just by winning. We earn respect by constantly battling for position, by fighting back, by never giving up, by being *mentally tough*, by giving it everything we've got.

President Dwight D. Eisenhower put it well: "It's not about the size of the dog in the fight; it's about the size of the fight in the dog."

To be a clutch competitor, all of us must surpass our genetics and upbringings. We must learn how to override our primal competitive responses and fight back.

Stay with me here. Typically, our Big Dog goes over the top, while our Little Dog doesn't show up; our Big Dog underestimates our opponents, while our Little Dog overestimates our opponents; our Big Dog is shocked when we lose, while Little Dog is shocked when we win. Both of our Dogs have detrimental *primal behaviors* that require wise, assertive control to perform well in competition.

Can't you see those basic competitive archetypes represented on the Grr Meter in the *Override* illustration on the previous page? Those who are under Grred up and timid as well as those who are over Grred up and angry. Very few competitors have learned how to control their Dogs and remain balanced, focused, and confident throughout the emotional ups and downs of a tournament.

I hope you timid Little Dogs are realizing that the reason you're a Little Dog is because *you think* you're a Little Dog. Each of us, every single one of us has a Big Dog deep inside. Once you Little Dogs realize that your Big Dogs are just waiting to come out and assert themselves, your whole world will change.

Also, I hope you overly aggressive Big Dogs realize that being angry is not being focused or determined, it's just being angry. Anger does not promote rational thought and solid execution.

Understanding our basic genetics and our upbringing influences helps shed some light on our current competitive attitude, which is a starting point. Then, if tackled with a little passion, you can become more of the competitor you want to be, one who can override Doubt Demon nonsense, handle the pressure, and have reliable confidence at your core.

Work Myth

To further explain how to obtain a fierce competitive attitude, the key ingredient to winning, we need to revisit one of our missions, which is to break the physical-work-builds-confidence myth.

It's generally accepted in the athletic community, especially at the youth and high school levels, that hard physical work translates into competition confidence. Respectfully, I disagree. I have known countless athletes of all ages who have worked as hard as anyone, on and off the course and yet still fall apart emotionally when it's tournament time. If hard physical work were all that was necessary to win, many more players would be champions.

It's a misconception to think that hard physical work translates into mental toughness or competition confidence. In weightlifting, doing set after set, day after day, is a mental grind, but it's not mental toughness. That's training hard. I think the lines have been blurred.

Mental Toughness scenes (above) depict just a few of the situations that require emotional balance: sports, the classroom, and countless social encounters. Get real and know how and why you react to any kind of challenge, then, fire up your left brain to step out and take a risk with confidence.

Override Doubt Demon non-sense by controlling your emotional reactions—of course you're nervous.

Yes, successful competitors must develop a work ethic that most people will not commit to; we must work hard physically and sacrifice. And yes, there is a certain mental drive that goes along with the endless practicing to build the variety of swing skills and the physical conditioning necessary for high-stakes golf. But that's not mental toughness, that's just not being a physical wimp.

Just as we need to separate practice from competition, we need to separate physical toughness from mental toughness—they are entirely different. Sure, training hard is part of our mental drive, but overcoming physical pain and fatigue has very little to do with managing doubt attacks under pressure.

Don't misunderstand me; I'm not suggesting that hard physical work is not a vital ingredient to being a successful competitor. It definitely is, and it certainly helps in the Grr-building department, but that's only half of the equation. Rigorous, reflective mental work is also required to walk out of state or nationals a champion.

At state- and national-level competitions, all of the top-ranked athletes have worked hard—physically. It's the athletes who have also worked hard mentally who prevail. No matter how good you feel about your swing, add an element of pressure and most of us shrink. Hard, relentless physical work is important, but thinking that it translates into mental toughness and competition confidence is a myth.

Mental Toughness

Mental toughness in not just about emotional control, it also includes grappling with self-evaluation—how one views oneself. Not feels, *views.* There is a substantial difference. *Feeling* is an emotional opinion as opposed to *viewing,* which is rational, objective reality. The harshness comes from seeing who we truly are, versus who we are projecting.

Stop for a second and pretend you're playing in a televised tournament where the cameras are following you around. The commentators are talking about your physical skills, but what's more telling is that they're talking about your confidence for every stroke you take. Think about what they'd be saying about you. How would they be describing your confidence and your execution? Not your swing—your Grr factor. That's how you should view yourself, which is reality, not fantasy.

Evaluating ourselves mentally is far scarier territory than evaluating ourselves physically, especially in the twenty-first century. Why? Look around. How many people do you know that truly hold themselves accountable instead of always making excuses? How many of your peers really work hard in school or at work, trying to excel? How many of your friends want success without the discipline, commitment, and the blood, sweat, and tears required to achieve it?

Evaluating ourselves truthfully is not a common cultural occurrence, and thus is a mindbender of a task. To be truly great at any sport, you must know which side of your brain is controlling the thinking—which controls the body, which controls the club, which in turn controls whether or not you win.

Make sense? Mental toughness is being able to see our doubts, fears, and psychological weaknesses, admit them, and then overcome them. The toughness part is accepting the truth and not avoiding it.

The great thing is that when we're able to get out of our own way and use the tremendous emotional energy, which we all have in competition, our physical skills can take over. That mental state is often referred to as "the zone," where crisp execution feels almost effortless and is an experi-

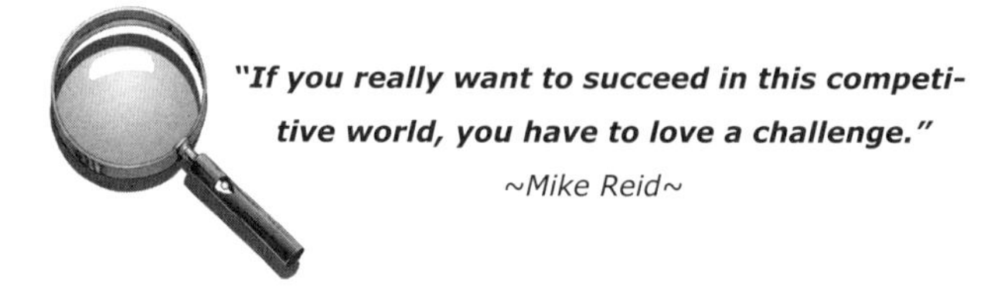

ence we never forget. To achieve that state takes a combination of physical and mental toughness.

It's obvious to me that we'll never find the zone with our Little Dog in control—worried, shaking, and doubtful. We only find the zone by submitting our Little Dog and unleashing our Big Dog—the part of us that wants to compete and win.

So Grr up, don't run away from the truth. You're beginning the simple process of gaining insight into your competitive self.

Enter the Cave

Entering the Cave of Reflection for the first time is intimidating and takes guts; a Grred-up attitude that Little Dogs squirm over. Younger or older, discovering our primal competitive response can be an intimidating proposition. However, as competitors we have no choice. We must go inside the Cave of Reflection and address the question chiseled on the wall over the Pool of Power: *Why can you believe?*

Not very many of us seek the answer to that question, because what we believe becomes who we are. In other words, when you're under pressure, are the bulk of your thoughts negative or positive? Do you believe you can make the shot or do you clutter your mind with negative garbage? For the majority of you, the answer is the latter, which is why your core is doubtful, not confident, and why you can't answer the *why can you believe?* question with any clarity. Hopefully, you're starting to see how to change that.

Discovering your primal competitive response is not hard if you're willing to be truthful and to look beyond the image you project. The metaphoric Cave of Reflection helps us separate our real selves from our projected, fantasy selves.

We all project, walking around trying to look all confident and powerful or timid and weak or something in between. We manipulate the projection to get what we want in specific situations. If you think about it, you know exactly what I'm talking about. A lot of us trick ourselves (and others)

The Cave of Reflection (right) can be intimidating, but once we see that our fears are self made and not as scary as we thought, we can take charge of our emotional reactions to pressure. Do you see the 3 Doubt Demons waiting just inside the entrance? Grr up and go inside.

CAVE
OF
REFLECTION

into believing we're Big Dogs, but when a real challenge presents itself, we crumble and crash. Or we project a timid and submissive personality, but when a real challenge presents itself, we shed that projection and kick butt—we let our Big Dogs out.

Once inside the Cave, take a long look in the *Pool of Power* as illustrated to the right. Look honestly at your primal reactions. Picture the Grr Meter and where you naturally fit. Do you fight, flee, or freeze, and to what degree? Relax, nobody will know your honest reflective thoughts unless you want them to, but it's important that you know, because insight reveals knowledge, and knowledge equals power—*competitive power.*

Primal responses to threat are not the same for everyone. It's not one size fits all; it's very individual and personal. The nervous emotion associated with pressure situations can be paralyzing for some, but exciting for others. How do you respond? Obviously those who find it exciting have an advantage. Why? Doubt is a reality that a competitor has to live with for an entire career. Intimidation, hesitation, distraction, confusion, and a hundred other negative descriptors are part of being a competitor; it's just the way it is.

So don't deny it. Do your best to understand how you react to threatening situations of any kind—whether you're a confronter or an avoider. If you're an avoider, how can you expect to confront the Doubt Demons or a fierce competitor? You can't.

The good news is, when we're open and aware, we're able to look our Doubt Demons square in the eyes, understand them, override them, and silence them. Otherwise, our Demons grab us by the throat and suck the oxygen right out of us. It's like committing competitive suicide because we're doing it to ourselves. To detect doubt triggers as they are happening, we must know where they are coming from. Then, we can fight back with *mental toughness* and use that amazing competition energy to our advantage.

Detect It

Detecting a meltdown before reaching the critical point is easy to do when we're emotionally intelligent and truthful with ourselves.

A commonly missed point is that when we feel dominant, doubt and intimidation are not an issue. It's when we feel inferior or uncer-

The Pool of Power (above), inside the Cave of Reflection, doesn't lie; it reflects our true competitive nature, our PCR. Consider this: If we wince at looking at our competitive self, how can we expect to answer the "Why can you believe?" question?

tain that doubt, intimidation, and distraction become major obstacles in ourability to perform.

Those reactions are completely natural. When something triggers feelings of insecurity our two brains, "I can't" and "I can," get into the confidence battle. We flip-flop back and forth from confident to doubtful, especially when the pressure is on and we really want to succeed. But keep in mind that doubt triggers are not pressure. Pressure is something else. In a pressure situation, if we're up against an opponent we know we can beat, we're licking our chops for the opportunity to shine. The little voice in our head is saying, "Bring it on." Even though there's still pressure to perform, doubt is not in the picture. When we *feel* superior, which is based on concrete reasons we can list, we're full of confidence. But for whatever reason, when we feel inferior and pressure is added—BAM!—we melt down emotionally.

Detecting doubt is as simple as identifying any other emotion. We know when we're happy, sad, or angry. Doubt is no different. The problem is that when it comes to doubt, we often hide from it or deny that it exists.

Overriding doubt requires anticipating it and welcoming it. Being truthful with ourselves and saying, "I'm nervous, scared, intimated, shaken to the core," whatever it may be, and then laughing it off and talking ourselves down—sort of a "duh" moment—"Of course I'm nervous, I'm in a tournament and everyone's watching, so let's get over this and go kick some butt."

Talking Yourself Down

When competing, if your 3F response is to run for cover and hide, to avoid confrontation, you might be a "jumper." I use this metaphor because sometimes jumpers can be talked down from their emotionally exaggerated state, from the Monkey Mode ledge. Competitors melting down are in a similar emotional situation; their minds are dominated by thoughts of embarrassment, inadequacy, and failure. Negative "what if" scenarios of what might go wrong take hold, which can result in utter despair.

To successfully battle intense pressure, override doubt and then answer the "why can you believe?" question with tangible, positive descriptors. Say to yourself, "I'm not afraid of the spotlight, I have a great golf swing, and I've made this shot before, so *watch this*!"

Chapter 5 will teach you more about this LBi technique, which is much more than positive thinking or imagining what you want to happen. With

Photo: San Deigo State's Adam Porzak prepares for his next shot as he walks up a fairway at the Mountain West Conference Men's Golf Championship, Tucson, Arizona. *Trevor Brown, Jr./ NCAA Photos*

SDSU
SAN DIEGO
STATE
Adam Po

LBi skills, you'll be able to *replace* feelings of panic with actual memories of when you Grred up, were assertive and successful.

Welcome It

Now that you are discovering your real competitive self, the obvious next step is recognizing and welcoming the butterflies, the doubt, the nerves, and the apprehension.

Here's a personal doubt story. In 1983 I was competing in the US Senior National Powerlifting Championships, which at the time was the most competitive tournament of the year, even more competitive than the world championships.

I lifted in the 181-pound weight class and was in the best shape of my career. In a powerlifting competition, the squat is the first lift. I was planning on attempting a personal record, which at the time was only a few pounds off a world record.

Nationals were being held in a huge arena with a few thousand people attending. In powerlifting you get three attempts on platform; the first two are basically warm-ups. When your name is called you have three minutes to execute the lift or you're disqualified. My first squat attempt at 644 pounds was easy. My second attempt at 683 pounds was incredibly solid—I felt great. I picked 722 pounds for my third and final attempt.

As I walked on and took control of the platform I was in a great place mentally. I was totally confident—or so I thought. As I ducked under the bar a little voice from demon land said, "You're going to fail," and along with the negative voice came this mental video of me taking the weight out of the rack, my legs breaking off at the knees, and the weight driving me straight down through the platform.

This obviously broke my concentration. I looked up and actually laughed out loud. It startled me, and it came from nowhere. I backed away from the weight, took a couple of deep breaths and told the little demon voice where to go. As I approached the bar the second time, I fought back the negativity with real feelings from my solid warm-ups and numerous memories of successful big lifts in the past. Doubt resurfaced slightly, but Grred up and focused I plowed ahead.

I made the lift, and in doing so set an Oregon state record that still stands today.

What's the moral of the story? Doubt and intimidation will surface at the worst possible times. Being able to welcome and deal with the emotional turbulence during critical moments is what makes a competitor clutch. A clutch competitor has the skills and core belief to look intimidation square in the face, smile and say, "Oh yeah, watch this!"

Override It

No matter what our typical reaction to confrontation may be, all of us must override it and *get some attitude.* A mentally tough Big Dog competitor does not care if his adversary is ten feet tall and stronger than steel. Without blinking, our Big Dog self will step up under any circumstances and execute, which is completely about attitude and skills.

Think of it like breaking boards in martial arts. A beginning student can't even break one board. Then, in a short time he can break three, then five, and then seven. What happens? The student not only learns better physical techniques, like using his hips and legs and striking the board squarely, but more importantly the student learns how to summon his power, to believe and penetrate, striking *through* the board.

That example also applies to competitive golf. Effective performances are about confidently striking the ball, placing the ball where you want it. It's not about trying—it's about doing. When you don't believe, you hesitate and end up short, long, or off line. It's a cause-and-effect relationship. If a martial arts student hesitates while trying to break five boards, he will break his knuckles. A warrior doesn't try to defeat the dragon—he slays it. No matter what, a competitor must command unflinching confidence that obliterates doubt and destroys hesitation—period!

Remember, our genetics and home environments do affect how we respond to difficulties, but those factors are just that, factors. If we're able to *override* Doubt Demon nonsense and then take control of our emotional reactions, our primal competitive response is irrelevant.

Through simple self-reflection, use of new language, and consistent mental rehearsal, all of us can improve our reactions to the spotlight. We can be more than just golfers, have more confidence under pressure, and be more fearsome, respected competitors.

So step out of your comfort zone and take risks; choose psychological danger, not safety. Be aware of anticipating your *super emotional* reactions either before or while they're happening, so you can override your primal competitive reactions, *get some attitude*, and execute with confidence.

CHAPTER 4

REVIEW

Override: Manage Your Primal Competitive Response

Summary

Poor mental performances are typically tied to doubt, distraction, and hesitation. *Overriding* Doubt Demon-induced "I can't" thinking is vital. The first step is to know our typical reaction to threat, our primal competitive response. Do you fight, flee, or freeze? Remember, our confidence is not limited or determined just by genetics. Competing successfully requires overriding the emotional drama and then knowing *why* you can believe. *Override*.

Test—What did you learn?

True/False Statements:

1) The 3 Doubt Demons are detectable.
2) Your level of confidence is only determined by your genetics.
3) Shy, timid athletes can never be assertive, confident competitors.
4) Mental toughness has nothing to do with self-reflection.

Do It!

Grr up and be brave, enter the Cave of Reflection, discover *your* primal competitive response and identify your doubt triggers. Make yourself aware, so you can mount a solid counter attack. Remember, life is your practice arena, so during emotionally challenging situations *override* the negative Grr reaction. Then, engage in rational self-talk to reduce doubt by recalling the many reasons *why* you can believe.

CHAPTER 5

REPLACE

Draw On **Success**

In this chapter you will learn how to *replace*—mental toughness skill #5—a skill that replaces the right brain's pessimistic whining and negative outlook with powerful, *push forward* memories of past Big Dog victories.

Our Big Dog self
can *replace* doubtful thoughts
with positive memories of
previous success.

Go ahead—give it your best shot—try to prove that your Big Dog doesn't exist. You can't do it. There are too many instances each and every day when you take a breath, suck it up, force yourself into psychologically difficult situations, and win. Hold up here, winning doesn't always involve a scoreboard; so redefining your definition of *win* is probably necessary.

For the majority of us doing something socially uncomfortable is an emotional challenge; it forces us out of our comfort zones. When we muster the courage and push forward and do it, that's when we win. Putting doubt aside requires rational thinking and attitude, which comes from our confident self—our Big Dog. Pushing forward is the winning part—the outcome is irrelevant, because being a Big Dog is in the *doing of it.*

Confirming that you have a confident self, and understanding what a confident/Big Dog moment really is, are prerequisites to using your newly developing competition mindset.

We all have a ton of Big Dog attitude deep inside, so the issue shifts to whether we can unleash it and have the skills to control it.

Check out this grandma story. Not my grandmother, but a grandmother. This took place in Colorado, early 2007. We've all heard the stories of the woman who lifted a car off her son to save his life—some serious Grr. But, since we didn't witness it, we question it. Well, this grandma story happened and was documented on the evening news.

Since I'm not trying to be a reporter, I'm probably going to mess up some of the details. So don't look too hard for the trees; connect with the larger point, the forest.

A stereotypical grandma and grandpa in their seventies are hiking in bear country—grizzly bear country. Unfortunately, the elderly couple crosses paths with a grizzly who decides Grandpa is going to be lunch. The bear attacks, has Grandpa by the throat—literally tasting blood—but Grandma decides … no way, bear, not today. Screaming over and over, "Fight back, don't give up" to her husband while ferociously thrashing the bear with a big stick, Grandma drives the bear off and saves their lives.

Cut to the hospital room. Grandpa's head, neck, shoulders and one arm are in bandages. He looks like a wounded soldier just returned from the battlefield. When asked what happened, he can only mutter, "She saved our lives; I gave up." Frail, gray-haired Grandma can't even relate to what she has done, and fiddling with a tissue in a weak, high voice whispers, "Well, sometimes we do what we must," while humbly looking to the floor.

Whatever Gram, you're a stud.

Grandma and Grandpa's bear encounter shows exactly why we are born with a ton of Grr: to assert our will. To fight back against threats, pain, hardship, and adversity—the list is long. Our Big Dog, our competitor, is where our passion and our Grr reside.

The problem is that in social situations Grr can quickly change from assertive to overly aggressive. And, like highly unstable plutonium, Grr is often associated with being out of control. So we avoid it rather than learn how to command and use it. But, to be a confident, successful competitor we must embrace our assertiveness and our Grr, which translates into attitude and drive. Attitude and drive exist in our Big Dog.

The point is we all have a Big Dog and it has a ton of Grr. The task is to find it and to learn how to use it.

Open Minds

"Minds are like parachutes, they only work when they're open." — Sir James Dewar, Scientist

Our Little Dog mind is closed, ultra self-conscious, and blocks learning. Our Little Dog dwells on negativity, complains, and melts down emotionally. In complete contrast, our Big Dog mind is open, self-determined, re-

The Spotlight (right) is a fun example of how the heat of the moment exposes two types of athletes: Those who are mentally unprepared and melt under the lights vs. those who are mentally well prepared and are rock solid under the lights.

COMPETITION
© 2010 Let's Win
HOPE
SWITCH
NARROW
FUEL
DOUBT ALARM
OVERRIDE
REPLACE
BELIEVE

flective, objective, rational, and interested in learning. Our Big Dog doesn't make excuses, does learn from mistakes, and adapts and overcomes.

By keeping an open mind, you will more fully engage the Let's Win! mental toughness skills and techniques. Keeping an open mind will enhance and enlarge the reflective process that produces real confidence at your core—confidence you can rely on under pressure.

Memory Scales

Pause a minute and study the *Memory Scales* on pages 90 and 93. The intent of those illustrations is to show the differences between our Little Dog memories and our Big Dog memories. Flip back and forth. Each one of the athletic figures represents an actual memory, not a fantasy. Our Little Dog remembers mostly negative, doubtful experiences, either from our competitive or our social worlds.

Which Memory Scale do you identify with? Does your mind recall mostly Little Dog, negative reactions or Big Dog, push-forward-and-execute actions? For example, if you had to make a list of ten negative personal attributes and ten positive, which list would be the easiest to complete? My guess is most of you would not be able to complete the positive list, but could rattle off the negative list with ease. Am I right?

Be aware that part of discovering whether your mind is weighted negatively or positively is knowing the difference between a Little Dog meltdown and a Big Dog victory, so let's better define both.

Our Little Dog self under threat is the easiest to understand. Our Little Dog self cowers and runs away; it crumbles and submits to pressure of any kind; its first thought is always "I can't." Even though we have learned to not look intimidated on the outside, inside we're a mess. Our Little Dog reactions are almost completely irrational and always focused on the negative. Our Little Dog self is marked by pessimism, doubt, fear, confusion, and hesitation—pure Monkey Mode.

Big Dog Experiences (right) are when we are confronted with a scary, intimidating challenge, but overcome the nerves, apprehension and fear and push forward. These experiences start very early in life. What are some of your Big Dog experiences? Think!

BIG DOG EXPERIENCES

You are braver than you realize.

RIDING A BIKE
You may not remember learning to ride a bike, but can't you envision and feel the fear? Did you do it anyway?

A DIVING BOARD
Jumping off of anything is intimidating, especially when everyone is watching. Imagine what the kids waiting are saying, "Come on chicken."

FUND-RAISING
Stepping out from the group behind you, invading someone's space, and confronting them with a request is scary. But we push forward and do it anyway.

SNOWBOARDING
Starting down a mountain with a "yeehaw" takes guts and rational thinking, because our right brain is screaming, "Don't do it."

A DANCE
The possibility of rejection and humiliation is extreme, there's no way around it, but we Grr up and go for it.

LITTLE DOG MEMORIES
Our Little Dog remembers mostly negative experiences.
MEMORY SCALE
© 2010 Let's Win!
BIG DOG
"That was the worst game of my life. I totally suck!"
"Everyone was staring ... my legs felt like rubber."
"It was too windy... if only the weather wasn't so bad."
LITTLE DOG
"It was no use ... that guy always beats me."

The complete opposite are our Big Dog reactions and experiences. Keep in mind that a Big Dog moment is not when we win the trophy, even though that may happen. For example, if you happen to be the most skilled player at a tournament and win, how is that a Big Dog moment? It's not. Without serious pressure—real intimidation—followed by recovery and execution, there's no Big Dog moment.

A Big Dog victory is when we face an emotional challenge that requires us to Grr up, submit our Doubt Demons, push forward, and execute. A Big Dog moment is about emotionally winning *inside*—overcoming our hesitant reactions. Make sense? That's why even though we may not win the tournament, when we overcome fear and execute, we still feel somewhat fulfilled. Deep inside we know we gave it everything we had at that moment—*that's a Big Dog victory.*

There are more examples of real *Big Dog Experience* on page 89. Those are true Big Dog moments, and there are many others. This distinction between winning the trophy and defeating our Doubt Demons is the key to controlling our emotions under pressure.

Hopefully this broader definition of a Big Dog moment has stimulated your competitive, push-forward memories. Now let's dig into tipping your Memory Scale as far toward confident as we can by de-dramatizing your Little Dog memories and emphasizing your Big Dog memories, so you can draw on success and execute whenever and wherever you need to.

Replace: Mental Skill #5

Pause and take a close look at the steps and the scenes in *Replace: Mental Skill #5* on pages 96 and 97. To be clear, those scenes are not fantasies of what you would like to have happen, they are scenes that capture what actually *has* happened throughout your life. Those three scenes *are* Big Dog victories. You overcome doubt every day. The more details that you can clearly remember and hold fresh in your mind from

The Memory Scale Weighed Negative (left) shows how our Little Dog remembers mostly "I can't" experiences. Experiences when we were dominated by pessimism, confusion, and hesitation, and when we ran from the challenge and collapsed.

your Big Dog victory experiences, the more meaningful and usable those memories will become under pressure.

Remember, the skill you're learning is to *replace,* a skill that replaces negative, doubtful thinking with positive, successful memories. This skill process requires all of your Big Dog moments to be quickly and easily accessible. For example, where do you put your favorite shirts? Tucked way in the back of your closet or up front and easy to find? It's the same with your Big Dog, push-forward victories—keep 'em front and center in your mind.

As we walk through the following *Replace* steps (Recall, Feel, Save/Play), think of your competitive experiences with as much detail as possible. Relive the feelings and mental pictures that are tied to each experience, either from your sports life or your social life.

Step 1—Recall:

Hopefully you have some video of your past tournament performances. If not, do your best to remember specific competition experiences. We're going to recall two totally opposite competitive states: one when your Little Dog self was in control and you felt intimidated and small, and the other when your Big Dog self was in control and you felt confident and large.

First, let's analyze an intimidated Little Dog experience. It's important to start seeing those *negative* experiences from a different angle, to turn them into experiences that are highly educational and motivating. This isn't some kind of Jedi mind trick. When we can engage the logical side of our brain and see why we tremble, whether it's because of our primal competitive response (genetics and upbringing) or something else, we're able to change and *replace* that typical doubtful behavior.

Are you thinking of a Little Dog experience? Where was it? What happened? As you're reliving that experience, how do you feel? What's your internal reaction? Are you embarrassed? Hiding emotionally from yourself? Making excuses? Or, are you being truthful, accountable, and learning something? Does remembering that intimidating experience

The Memory Scale Weighted Positive (right) shows how our Big Dog remembers mostly "I can" experiences. Experiences when we were dominated by optimism, courage, and focus, and when we stepped up, took a risk, and confidently executed.

BIG DOG MEMORIES
Our Big Dog remembers mostly positive experiences.
© 2010 Let's Win!
"I really kicked some butt that day."
"Wind, rain, cold ... who cares."
"What crowd ... I had a job to do."
BIG DOG
"I could have beat that guy barefoot."

shrink you or motivate you? Don't look for physical mistakes or flawed technique. Take a serious look at your Little Dog self in action, the part of you that lacks confidence and always hesitates. Ask yourself questions like why was I so shaken? Why did I emotionally melt down? What was so intimidating?

Next, watch or recall a totally opposite performance, a performance when you unleashed your confident self and executed. Analyze your Big Dog moments by asking yourself (and answering) similar questions. Why were you confident? Why weren't you intimidated? "I don't know" is mentally lazy. Get to the bottom of *why* you felt the way you did. Vividly remember as many experiences as you can when you overcame intimidation and pushed forward.

The more details you're able to capture, the clearer and more usable that memory will become, which provides greater believability under pressure. Picture that experience and where you were at the time. It may have been on the range, just before you teed off, or on the turn after posting a solid front.

If you don't have very many push-forward moments from the sports world, import them from your social world where you have Big Dog victories every day—guaranteed.

Are you starting to see the differences between Little Dog meltdowns and Big Dog victories? Are you seeing both in your own life? It's relatively simple when your mind is open and you're willing to be real with yourself. Then, once we've gone through the process a few (hundred) times, you'll see a pattern develop: you're either intimidated or confident. There are degrees of feeling between these two extremes, of course, but we find ourselves in one or the other the majority of the time. In other words, we are rarely neutral or flatline.

Step 2—Feel:

Once you've relived your competitive experiences, reach deeper for the feelings—your emotions at that moment.

Try to actually relive your mental/emotional state before you pushed forward. Were you agitated, apprehensive, confused, disoriented, maybe even nauseated? Try to link up the feelings before and after, because each end is drastically different, just like the examples on the Grr Meter.

Note: Deeper thinking like you're engaging in right now is the tough part of mental skill building for two reasons: 1) Reflection takes emotional guts; and 2) Reflection requires full concentration, which requires mental stamina. Our minds dart here and there. It's hard to make our minds do what we want them to do for more than a few seconds. So if you're feeling a little foggy, that's brain fatigue. If necessary, take a mental recovery break. Give your mind a chance to organize and grow. You're literally building mental muscle. No kidding. Brains grow when required, just like muscle.

Be patient! When your mind wanders, just relax and bring it back on track. Controlling your thinking is similar to being in a class and realizing you've been drifting off and haven't heard a word, and bingo, you tune right back in. A similar example of a wandering mind is reading a page but not retaining much. Realize that a wandering mind during a high-stakes competition, most of the time, is devastating. Just force your mind to narrow focus and concentrate.

Back to Step 2—Feel: Your core confidence is only as solid as your confirmed Big Dog experiences, which are the only mental images you can truly believe in. The Memory Scales offer great examples of what we vividly remember.

Once you've analyzed and felt a Little Dog meltdown along with savoring a Big Dog victory, it's time to confirm them. This confirmation step is an important part of the process. It's like putting a stamp on it,

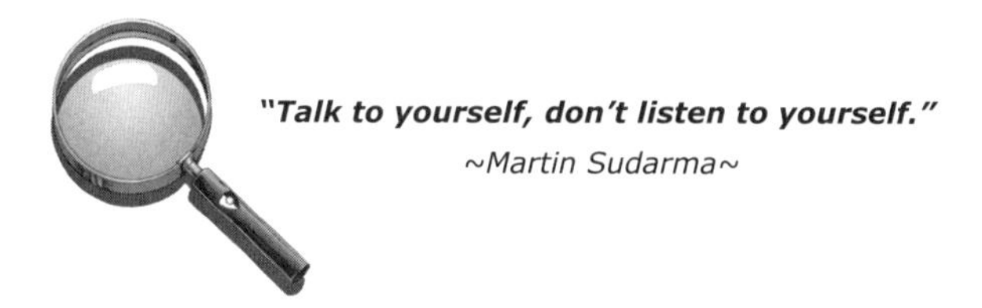

"Talk to yourself, don't listen to yourself."

~Martin Sudarma~

which makes it more real, lasting, and usable. Confirming is nothing more than being honest with yourself, "Yes, your honor, this is exactly what, how, and *why* it happened—honest."

Step 3—Save/Play:

Once you've formally confirmed both types of competitive experiences, it's time to save them. This is the fantasy part of the process, but don't dismiss it.

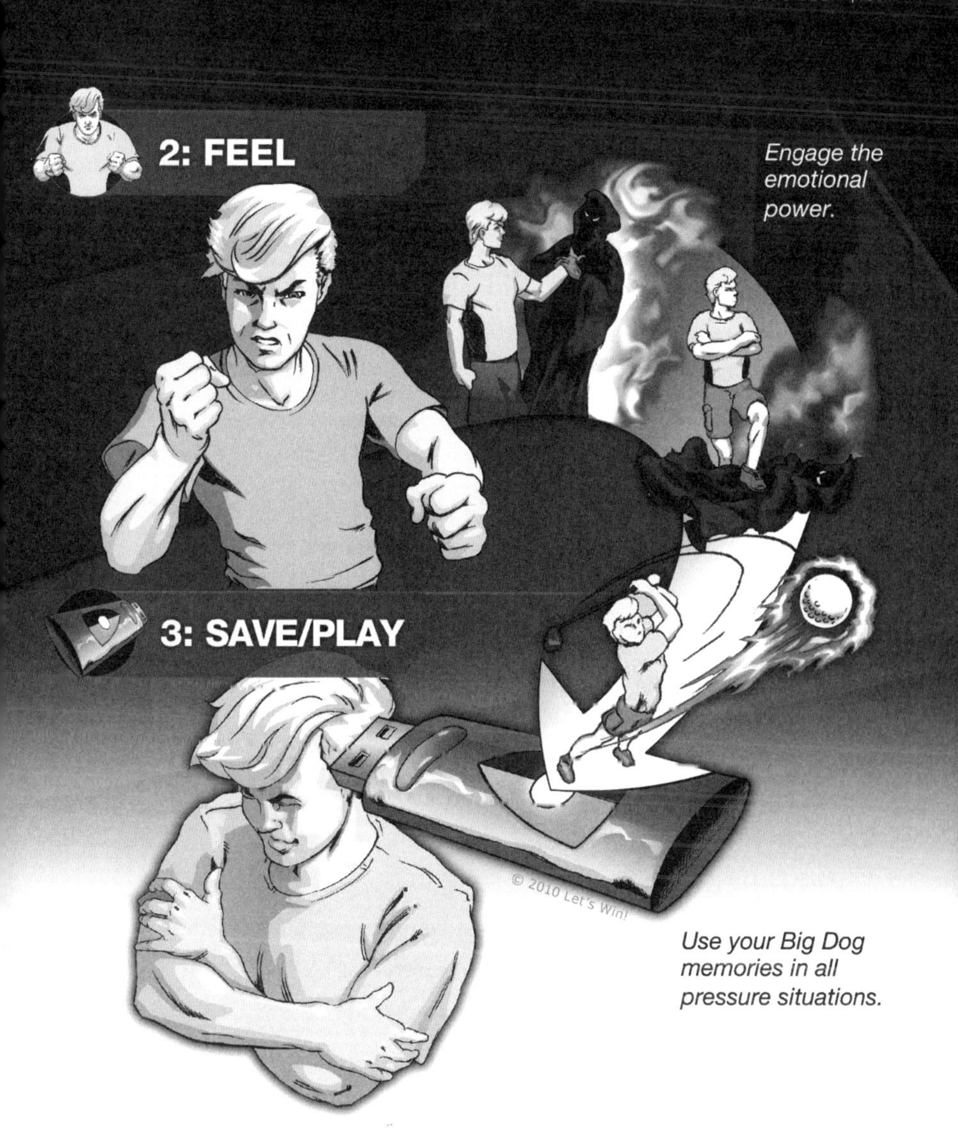

Be sure you understand this "mental storage device" idea, and somewhere in your mind save all of those important competition experiences just like you'd store files on a computer or food in the fridge or clothes in the closet. The goal of this entire mental toughness system is *believability under pressure*.

This save/play task is to figure out what kind of mental storage device is the most meaningful to you. Some of you may actually keep a real notebook.

Others may use a sort of mental flash stick drive, while others may think of burning a mental DVD.

Save your Big Dog memories in the front of your mind, to tip the Memory Scale toward confident and in your favor. You don't want to get caught searching your memories for reasons why you can believe when the Doubt Demons are banging down your door.

Are you seeing how this works? Quickly accessible positive memories stimulate the "been there, done that" response, which engages the rational side of our brain. Then, rather than allowing a threat response to get out of control, we're able to offer a controlled reaction to that moment's doubt trigger.

Your core confidence is based on *you believing in you*. That belief is based on whether you remember more positive than negative. Once you have mastered the recall process, you will be able to use this valuable replace skill in action, part of your arsenal of LIVE competition skills.

Before I break down 5 five key LIVE competition skills, let's talk about two methods you are probably already familiar with—visualization and positive mental attitude (PMA)—so the differences between those and the Let's Win! mental toughness skills are crystal clear.

Visualization & PMA

Visualization and PMA are the most common methods for dealing with high-stakes pressure. Both techniques have variations. In golf, the most common form of visualization is imagining a shot's shape, the swing necessary to produce the shape, and then seeing the imaginary shot's success. The premise is, when it's showtime and our brains are scrambled, if we visualize a shot mechanically, we just plug into that vision and muscle memory will take over.

The other common method to counter pressure-induced doubt is PMA, repeating positive statements, attempting to convince ourselves we're not really intimidated.

Yes, I'm oversimplifying, but when we break it down, those basic descriptions are accurate.

I never had much success managing doubt eruptions with either of those common methods, because they don't get at the root of the problem. We get intimidated in most of life's pressure situations and always will. Emotions and destructive thinking must be managed, not ignored or avoided.

Visualization and PMA can be somewhat productive, but clearly are not a complete set of Doubt Demon counterattack skills. Fighting the Doubt Demons successfully requires something more: the ability to think logically and muster some emotional intelligence. Visualizing shot shapes, swing mechanics, putting lines and pace, etc., are all good when we're practicing, between shots, or when fellow competitors are scoping out their shots. It's a useful mental activity; it gives our mind something to do rather than just scream in panic. And repeating positive statements is always positive. But riding our emotional brain's molten lava without melting takes a greater skillset than imagining or repeating. Visualization and PMA have their place, but dealing with our negative, hesitant, "I can't," super-emotional reactions requires a more direct, reliable plan of action. The LBi Technique is that more direct, reliable plan of action.

Save your Big Dog memories in the front of your mind, to tip the Memory Scale in your favor.

LBi Thinking

Throughout this book, one way or another, I circle back and point to how left-brain-integrated thinking is the only sure defense we have against Doubt Demon attacks. That's why we labeled our core technique or skill process LBi, for left-brain integration—an in-the-heat-of-the-moment thinking process that shifts our focus from doubtful and panicky to confident and composed.

LBi thinking promotes focused, objective, left-brain reasoning in contrast to irrational, unrestrained, right-brain outbursts.

In competition, LBi thinking is both sequential and circular. It's sequential because we utilize several primary skills: override, breathe, Grr up, replace, and believe. It's circular because Doubt Demon-fighting is constant; we repeat the LBi thinking sequence anticipating the next doubt trigger.

This may seem like a lot right now, but the significance of both thinking rationally and using LIVE competition skills will become apparent in no time—maybe within the next few minutes.

LIVE Competition Skills

First, let's go back and review two very important images from Chapter 1, the illustrations on pages 16 and 17, our left and right brains. Figuratively, those competing images represent our confident "I can" psychology and our scared "I can't" psychology; our Big Dog self and our Little Dog self; our assertive self and our fearful self. Those two primal responses to threat control our actions in one way or another. Our two minds are constantly battling for control, or in many cases not battling at all because our Little Dog has already won.

Keep in mind, our emotional right brain has a very loud voice. For most people, it is the dominant voice. Thinking rationally and using the LIVE competition skills illustrated on pages 104 and 105, adds an even louder, intentional, confident voice to all competitively threatening situations.

Now let's break down five key LIVE competition skills.

Skill 1—Override:

Being aware of and overriding persistent doubt triggers is the first step to preventing or recovering from an emotional meltdown. In tournament situations, it's very important to be constantly assessing where you are on the Grr Meter—to be anticipating and then openly acknowledging your emotional reactions—so you can override the negative ones.

Eventually, with practice, you'll know how to use your mental toughness skills to *override* your "I can't" psychology and its doubt triggers before it's too late.

Photo: A tough bunker shot tests the nerves at the Mountain West Conference Men's Golf Championship at the Catalina Course—Tucson National, in Tucson, Arizona. *Trevor Brown, Jr./NCAA Photos*

Replace what started the "I can't" meltdown cycle with vivid mental pictures of previous success.

For example, let's say that you're at a big tournament and catch a glimpse of the competition. Of course you're going to react. Your stomach knots and the Doubt Demons attack with a barrage of negative images of you and positive images of them. Or, if it's not your competitors that cause the reaction, something else will, such as the spectators, your personal performance expectations, or a visually intimidating hole. The list goes on and on. What do you do? Laugh to yourself, openly acknowledge the emotional reaction, and breathe. Override it!

Skill 2—Breathe:

Oxygen is one of those gotta-have kinds of things, so learning how to breathe as you're strangling yourself is very useful. The increased oxygen is calming and the rhythmic physical part induces a control response to your conscious mind, which translates into greater self-control overall.

The skill of deep, rhythmic breathing can be performed almost anywhere: sitting, standing, leaning, or lying down—in through your nose, out through your mouth. Slowly and steadily control the air flow in and out, holding at each end.

Pause and study the *Breathe* figures. Slowly inhale through your nose and as your lungs get to the full point, take in a little more. Then hold for three to five seconds. Purposely and slowly exhale through your mouth. Don't rush the exhale. Control the flow all the way to the last bit of air, then push out a little more. Now the really challenging part—don't gasp to take in a breath. Not even a quick little breath. Start inhaling slowly through your nose until your lungs are full again, which should take between three to five seconds. Hold when full, don't rush the exhale. Exhaling takes about the same amount of time as inhaling. Three to five seconds in both directions—the slower the better. Then repeat the cycle. It's amazing when you're able to control the start of inhaling and exhaling. At first you'll want to gasp for air (and probably will). That's okay. It's just a reflex that, once controlled, yields big results.

After several breathing-in-and-out cycles you'll feel relaxed and energized at the same time. The deep, rhythmic breathing skill is a very effective tool for many emotionally charged situations. Learn how to breathe, so you can Grr up.

Skill 3—Grr Up/Down:

When your emotions are demanding that you either drop your clubs and run or throw them in a burst of anger—opposite sides of the Grr Meter—you must kick in some LBi *before you can think.*

Chapter 4 dealt primarily with what Grr is, how to build it, and how to let your Big Dog out. So if you need to refresh your attitude files, now's a good time.

What's the best way to describe Grr? Growling should work.

Most everyone has been around a growling dog. Not a barking dog, a growling dog. The quiet, serious (not angry) growls are the kind I'm referring to.

For example, when a female with pups is lying with her head resting on a paw, and as you get to the edge of her comfort zone she gives you that low level growl that says, "Dude, one more step and we've got a problem." You stop right there. Why? That's serious Grr. The mother dog isn't messing around, it's not a game. We know she means business.

Better example: During Spartan times there were two groups of men—the Spartans and the ordinary. Can you imagine a Spartan's Grr, as opposed to an ordinary man's? Why would a butcher, baker, or candlestick maker need Grr? They wouldn't. Trust me, a true Spartan had the same attitude as the mother dog; there's no confusing their commitment to act on their warning—some serious Grr.

Can you growl? I mean seriously growl. Yes, this is intense. All of you pacifists need to get a grip. Competing, at its very core, is fundamentally assertive. And when our right brain is flashing all kinds of negative "what if"

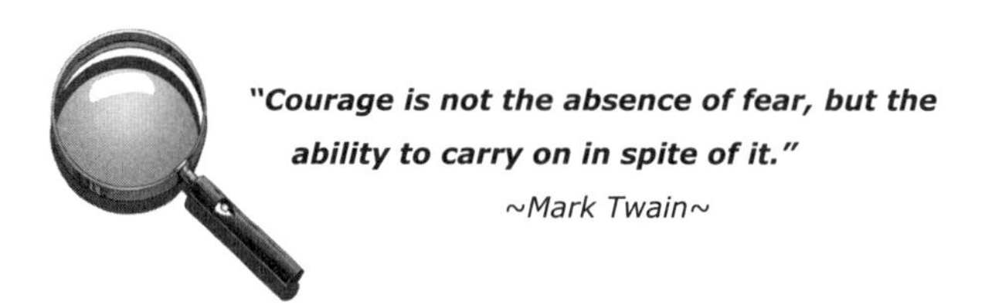

LIVE COMPETITION ROUTINES

Use the LIVE Competition Routines to prevent emotional meltdowns.

OVERRIDE

Heart Rate

Butterflies

Dry Mouth

Nausea

REACT TO DOUBT

BREATHE

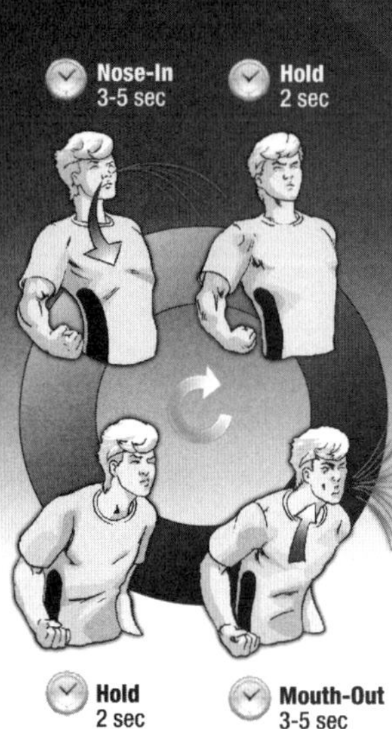

CALM THE NERVES

GRR UP

Serious eyes

Clenched teeth

Tight fists

Flexed abs

SWITCH TO OtherSelf

Use the ***LIVE Competition Routines*** (above) when it's time to perform and your emotions are bursting. Switch to your OtherSelf, breathe, override timidity and negativity, Grr up (or down), draw on success, and let your Big Dog out. Think! Be mentally active. Listen to your rational left brain and focus on the positive—*believe in your training.*

insanity, we must Grr up and replace that negative, destructive thinking. If you're an over-Grr type and often have to refrain from chucking your clubs in the water or strangling one of your opponents, Grring down is just as important as Grring up. You must be emotionally balanced before you can think rationally and replace.

DRAW ON SUCCESS

LET YOUR BIG DOG OUT

Skill 4—Replace:

As the Doubt Demons swarm and remind you of your weaknesses, past failures, and potential embarrassments, along with running a highlight video of your opponent's strengths, you must be able to *think in a rational manner* to remember all of your confirmed Big Dog victories.

That's the reason to go through the tedious *replace* process we discussed earlier—the process of recalling, feeling, and saving, so you can easily use your positive memories under pressure.

Envision thinking rationally in a sequence. We override doubt before getting tweaked, we kick in some LBi and some breathing, have serious Grr discussions with ourselves, and then replace whatever started the "I can't" meltdown cycle with our own positive, believable memories.

Breaking a severe meltdown cycle may require briefly shifting your focus to things you value, appreciate, and are familiar with: family, friends, a significant other, your education, your job, music, hobbies, the list goes on. Then, once you have put the drama in perspective—yeah it may be high-stakes, but not life or death—force your mind to think about the doubt trigger, breathe, and talk yourself down from the ledge. Engage your left brain, tell yourself *why* you can hit the fairway, stick the green, or make the putt.

That's not PMA. It's much more. Talking to yourself about *why* you can is not saying to yourself, "I can, I can, I can." Why you can is purposefully narrowing the self discussion to that shot, your solid mechanics, and then with memories of previous success pumping up your core confidence to make the shot. PMA is mindless repetition, where the replace skill is a rational, engaging, competent conversation about *why* you can believe. Otherwise, you're relying on hope.

Thinking objectively and replacing negative thinking enables you to *truly believe* in what you are about to do.

Skill 5—Believe:

Believing is not a natural, automatic occurrence, it must be forced; it requires diligent concentration. Yes, believing is a skill.

As you successfully defend against one doubt attack during a tournament, another is right behind. It's not over until the last putt is struck. You must remain on high alert until you're shaking hands on the 18th. Stay on guard and in the moment, rather than mentally drifting off thinking you're money and then getting hammered with a doubt trigger when you least expect it.

In competition, LBi thinking is circular. As doubt triggers morph from moment to moment and shot to shot, we repeat the sequence. Triggers must be anticipated or detected to be countered. That is why competing is mentally so exhausting. It takes volumes of oxygen, huge LBi thinking, and balanced Grr to manage our Dogs under pressure, especially if our typical primal competitive response is "I can't" oriented. But, once we develop fundamental emotional intelligence that forces rational thinking, we're able to draw on success, *believe*, and use our competitive emotions to our advantage.

Auto Competition Mindset

An auto competition mindset, being able to think clearly and competently under pressure, is similar to developing a physical skill that required practicing over and over until you got it right, the movement felt natural, and eventually you could do it whenever you wanted. Have patience—being able to override super emotions and replace negative thinking takes time and repetition. Expect to invest the same kind of determination and persistence that you've put into your swing, because without mental skills, you'll never reach your full competitive potential, period.

Engage your left brain, tell yourself why you can hit the fairway, stick the green, or make the putt.

Diligently practice your mental drills and activities to increase your core confidence. Think. Think about your competition mindset. Think about how to handle the pressure differently. Like swing skills, if you practice a little every day, you'll be able to neutralize crushing negativity in no time. You'll transform "I can't" reactions into "I can" actions.

Be ultra-patient and work at it.

Believe It

There are many pressure situations where you will be able to react and use the Let's Win! mental toughness skills to better manage your emotional reactions under pressure. Examples in both sport and social situations are endless. It's your first year on the team and every day you feel a little intimidated; or, you're off at a camp and matched up with some great talent and every moment seems like show time; or, you want to make the travel team and the competition is tough.

During any of those *threatening* situations, when you don't want to look bad and get nervous, force your mind to think and focus. Remember why you're doing what you're doing, get lots of air, and *replace* feelings of pessimism, doubt, and intimidation with all of your confirmed Big Dog success.

Another example is when you're lying in bed, nights before a big tournament, and feel the butterflies. To get a good night's rest when your emotions are churning, kick in some LBi thinking and use the PRE competition skills from Chapter 2.

Remember, when your emotional brain is screaming negative nonsense, you must come to your own defense. You win the confidence battle by replacing emotional drama with knowing *why* you can believe, which is based on concrete, definable reasons.

Trust me, the sky is not falling down and you're a braver and a much better competitor then you realize. So replace gloomy right-brain thinking and focus on your great mechanics and all of your previous success. Step up with real confidence, welcome the spotlight, let them stare, and pull the trigger.

You're good. Believe it!

CHAPTER 5

REVIEW

Replace: Draw On Success

Summary

We practice physical skills until we're sore and blistered, because our bodies need the extreme repetition. Our minds are no different. Practice the LBi technique and the LIVE competition skills to positively react to non-stop Doubt Demon attacks. We must be able to think, fight back, and *replace* negative thinking or we're toast.

Test—What did you learn?

True/False Statements:

1) A Big Dog moment is only when we win the trophy.
2) LBi thinking is a repetition of positive statements.
3) Our emotional right brain has a very loud voice.
4) Weighting our Memory Scale positive is essential.

Do It!

Life is emotionally challenging. Some people aren't so nice, and most of us are very self-conscious—start recognizing and anticipating *those* situations. When you feel nervous, anxious, afraid, angry, defensive, or irritated, use LBi thinking and *replace* the nerves to better handle that encounter. Amaze yourself by showing greater emotional control under pressure.

CHAPTER 6

BELIEVE

Let Your **Big Dog** Out

In this chapter you will learn how to *believe*—mental toughness skill #6—a competition skill that incorporates all of the other skills for whenever the Doubt Demons attack, allowing us to think rationally, to conquer doubt, and to draw on success.

Our Big Dog self
clearly knows *why* we can believe
in ourselves as we face the
greatest of pressure.

Now it's time to play some golf. All the preparation is behind you. You're on the range warming up—waiting. You feel confident, but uncertain. You don't know how sharp you'll be until you step onto the 1st hole and take your first swing. Now the real battle begins. The confidence battle—the battle between logic and emotion—the battle between your Little Dog self and your Big Dog self.

The previous chapters helped broaden your understanding of how to transform from a mere participant into a real competitor, in theory. Now we've come to the *do it* part.

First, let's summarize what you've learned. You've learned that *switching* from agreeable and modest to assertive and bold is essential. You've learned that *narrowing* your concentration to shot requirements, swing keys, and positive triggers is how to conquer the intensity of any competitive environment. You've learned that *fueling* for performance, rather than just eating to please your tongue is how to maintain thinking power for an entire round. You've entered the Cave of Reflection and can now *override* a Doubt Demon attack, because you know your competitive self better. You've learned how to *replace* emotional drama by using the LBi technique and then engaging in rational self-talk. Overall, you have learned several fundamental mental toughness skills on how to compete *mentally*. Now you're going to learn how to use all those skills at once, to let your Big Dog out and believe in yourself as the Doubt Demons attempt to destroy your confidence.

Remember, everything in this book has one purpose: to help you win the confidence battle, overcoming fearful hesitation when every nerve ending and all your emotions are screaming "I can't" and "I can" at the same time. The goal is to help you *believe* in yourself under the most extreme pressure.

Before we move on to the *do it* process of controlling your thinking during several nervy stages of a competition, I need to clarify composure, explain the "three-part thinking loop," expand drawing on success, and highlight a phase of Navy Seal training that illuminates how mental toughness skills are what the *real* Big Dogs use to defeat the Doubt Demons when it's all on the line.

Composure

The 3 Doubt Demons know our deepest fears and inhibitions, and are constantly plotting and planning. Check out the illustration to the right. Read the caption. Maintaining composure is about defeating those guys. Then, we can defeat our real opponents.

Clarifying composure is necessary, because when we hear the term composure, we usually think of staying calm during extreme emotional adversity. But is staying calm the goal? This is important, because words define how we think, and how we think determines how we behave.

Clarification is required because composure is a very common term. And we will never be calm in battle, ever. Focused, confident, assertive? Sure. Not freaking out? Definitely. Calm? Never. So don't think being calm is the goal, though many competitors do. As if at some point we will possess the emotional control to be calm in an intensely competitive environment. I don't think so. The goal is not to be calm; the goal is to use that intense, nervous competition energy to your advantage.

Competing successfully is about composure, the poised and balanced part of the definition. So from this point forward, think of composure as being poised and balanced, not calm.

Believe: Mental Skill #6

Take a look at the thinking examples on page 116. Hopefully, it's becoming clear that solid execution under any kind of pressure is about what you're thinking about at that time. Core confidence comes from letting your Big Dog out and by using all of the Let's Win! mental toughness skills, so you

The 3 Doubt Demons (right) love to mess with our innermost doubts and fears—notice the list. Those may not be your specific fears, but you have them, and they are what get in your way. The 3 Doubt Demons' only job is to constantly remind you of what unnerves you most, but now you don't have to listen.

Demon of
EMBARRASSMENT
Attacks you with fears of being laughed at.

Demon of
INADEQUACY
Makes you feel small, inferior, and intimidated.

Demon of
PAST FAILURE
Reminds you of all of your worst performances.

can *think*. But until we train our rational left brain to be more active under pressure, our emotional right brain has a much louder voice. This is why so many competitors get lost in negative "what if" emotional chatter that is not only unproductive, but is also the champion destroyer.

As you and your opponents work your way around the course, you're either concentrating on shot requirements, swing keys, and your successful memories, or you're mentally scattered, dwelling on negative "the sky is falling down" emotional insanity.

Under pressure, during threatening situations of any kind, our right brain streams one irrational thought/feeling after another:

"What if I hesitate?"

"What if he makes that shot?"

"What if I yank it OB?"

"What if I fan this putt?"

Blah, blah, blah. If your emotional brain remains dominant, you'll see all sorts of negative, undesirable consequences. You'll blow the shot, then the round, let your team down, lose the scholarship, and life as you know it will end. Those, and many other examples of negative "what if" emotional drama, equal pure Monkey Mode.

By now, you know your Little Dog self is doing all of the negative, destructive thinking, right? On the other hand, your Big Dog self is not interested in negative anything. When your Big Dog self engages in "what if" thinking, it's going to be positive. You'll see yourself confidently confronting the challenges of a visually intimidating course, boldly executing treacherous shots, winning the tournament, and then holding the championship trophy high over your head.

In order to believe, you must *choose* what to think about. Yes, choose, rather than just emotionally react. Solid execution comes from believing, and believing comes from using all the other skills so you can think rationally and choose which dog to listen to.

Believing is a forced, sequential thinking process; it's not automatic. Picture believing as a three-part thinking loop: shot requirements, swing keys, and previous success. Repeat the sequence and nothing else, absolutely nothing else. The power to believe is generated by *narrowing* to *that* shot's requirements, plugging into your swing keys, and vividly remembering previous success. Then, draw on the believability that is generated from accessing all those genuine mental pictures and block out everything else.

Photo: Rickie Fowler of the Oklahoma State Cowboys, watches his tee shot on No. 13, at the U.S. Amateur, Round 64. *TracyWilcox/ Golfweek.com*

Example: I have interviewed numerous state champions, across all sports, and only a couple of them have instinctively got it. A freshman D1 soccer player, a striker (scorer), put it best when I asked, "What do you think about before a big game or a big play?" "That's easy," he replied, "I think about all of the times I've scored, in detail." The tone and the conviction in his voice were the telling aspects; they were clear, forceful, and believable. Those success memories provided serious personal power for him. And they will for you as well.

The bottom line is, a competitor's power comes from thinking rationally and drawing on previous success. Thinking rationally and drawing on success is how you answer the question "why can you make the shot?" Because you know the shot, you have the swing to

Believe—mental skill #6. Under pressure, use all of the skills to think with your assertive, competition mindset. Think rationally. React. Fight back. Know why you can believe and you will, so believe!

execute the shot, and you've done it before a hundred times, so you know you can do it again.

Those thoughts and feelings are what run through our minds when there's no pressure. The trick is learning how to *do it* under the competitive microscope. Think. Believe in yourself. Draw on success.

COMPETITION MINDSET THOUGHTS

Drawing On Success

The battle over whether you can or you can't occurs on a moment-to-moment basis, changing with each shot. The more fun you have battling the Doubt Demons and not freezing up, the better you will perform. It's a very fine line we competitors must tiptoe, so why not have fun and enjoy the moment?

Remember, the 3 Doubt Demons know your fears and will relentlessly push your buttons, attempting to convince you that you don't have what it takes. The Demon of Past Failure will run a highlight reel of all the shots you've missed; the Demon of Inadequacy will whisper you're too short, too slow, too weak, too inexperienced, too *something;* and the Demon of Embarrassment will flash mental pictures of all kinds of humiliating outcomes.

Overcoming senseless "the sky is falling down" Doubt Demon chatter is done by listening to your left brain's contrasting voice say, "Whatever, that's all bull. You've made this shot many times before, so let's do this,—you're good."

Note that some *replace* discussions are a bit more aggressive, the language is a bit harsher. Sometimes we need to smack ourselves around a bit to knock some sense—logic—into our fearful, intimidated mindsets. Then, once you get your left brain fired up, to maintain a positive, believing outlook, lock on to the numerous memories of success and the positive feelings associated with them.

Knowing how to draw on success is essential, because Doubt Demon drama is relentless and unavoidable. That's why *rehearsing* crashing is important, so we have a *go-to* process for recovery. Knowing how to think rationally and how to draw on success is the only way to consistently perform well at a high level.

Navy Seal Training

Whoa! Navy Seal training—talk about the need to have a response to overcome fear and intimidation. Navy Seal methods for this are similar in many ways to the Let's Win! mental toughness skills, even though we didn't get our skills from them and they didn't get theirs from us.

To become a Seal, one must pass several competencies. The third competency, the water competency, is the best example of utilizing mental toughness skills to not freak out under extreme threat.

The primary Seal concern is that if you *can't think* during life or death situations, you will jeopardize both yourself and your team. The water competency ordeal quickly brings to the surface (literally) those who are not capable of thinking under serious threat. I mean extreme threat.

Check this out: Picture a huge pool about fifteen feet deep, with a surface area at least the size of a basketball court. The sides of the pool are far away when you're out in the middle.

A recruit is equipped with a scuba mask, flippers, and a mouth piece with hoses connected to an air apparatus on his back. In the water along with the recruit are several Seal instructors with bad intentions.

The bottom line is, a competitor's power comes from thinking rationally and drawing on previous success.

To pass water competency, a recruit must stay submerged for twenty minutes, never surfacing, while the Seal instructors mess with him from all angles: right, left, behind, above, and below. One instructor is pulling on the mask, while another is messing with the air hose. Right when the recruit gets the equipment back in place and is able to take a breath, BAM! another attack from a different angle. The intent of the relentless attacks is to simulate drowning and to determine a recruit's freak-out response. Can he stay composed and think or does he emotionally come unglued and need to surface?

If a recruit surfaces before the twenty minutes are up, he fails. Recruits get four attempts, and 77% of recruits fail all four of them. Failing means exiting Seal training. Talk about pressure.

After failing the first attempt, recruits are sent to mental toughness classes to learn how to talk themselves down. The intent of the mental toughness training is to help them control their emotions, allowing them to think their way through the confrontation. Emotional control is obviously critical on the battlefield.

Important note: For all of you get-fired-up, pound-your-chest, ra-ra, Hooyah types, note that the Seal recruits were not sent to inspiration class or learn-how-to-fight class, they were sent to learn how-to-*think*-under-pressure class. I'm not doggin inspiration and the associated revved up feelings, but I'm putting them in perspective. Inspiration may get us going, but rational thinking is what we use to execute what we are inspired to do.

In passing water competency, recruits demonstrate their ability to not panic under extreme threat, and in doing so, take one more step toward becoming a Navy Seal.

To be a consistently successful competitor, to believe in yourself when it's all on the line, you must be able to keep from panicing under threat too.

Competition Dos and Don'ts

All experienced competitors know that game plans only work until the first swing. After that, we must be able to adapt and overcome both mentally and emotionally.

The majority of Seal recruits fail water competency the first time. Those that pass in the remaining attempts learn how to override their "I'm gonna die" response by using *thinking skills* that they can rely on and believe in.

Any public competition has a similar, yet not as intense, primal survival reaction. As mentally tough Big Dog competitors, we use LIVE competition skills to adapt and overcome, to perform under pressure. We choose what to think about, increasing our emotional control, so we can physically perform to our full potential.

Pause and take a look at the illustrations on the following pages, *The Competition Dos and Don'ts*; the six nervy stages before and during a competition. The dos and don'ts offered in the illustrations are intended for quick reference later. The following is an expanded discussion of the night before, the morning of, the bus ride, the driving range, teeing off, and the critical finishing holes.

The Night Before:

The night before a tournament is all about getting a good night's sleep, which can be a difficult task when the stakes are high, the competition is stacked, and you want to perform your best. Your mind races and emotions surge from moment to moment. The night before, or for the big tournaments several nights before, is when you must start purposefully controlling your thinking to quiet your emotions.

When necessary, use the *breathing* skill to get lots of air, while thinking about your great mechanics in detail. Enlist all of the confirmed posi-

Photo: Junior Lion Kim focuses intently on one of the most difficult shots on golf: a short, in the heavy rough, no green to work with, chip shot at the NCAA Men's Golf Championships. *Lon Horwedel/MLive*

COMPETITION DOs & DON'Ts

THE NIGHT BEFORE

DO

Do your best to relax and enjoy the moment. Get lost in casual activities that you normally do. Do things that support *your* needs as a competitor.

DON'T

Don't dwell on tomorrow; that drama will come soon enough. Don't waste any of that special excitement (energy) that comes with the thrill of the unknown; it's time to be selfish.

tive memories you stored. Sure you might think about the course and how you're going to attack each hole, but that's not "what if" drama, that's strategizing.

The night before is the time to let go of everything, no matter what level of a tournament or which round it may be. Do your best to enjoy that moment. Quiet all of the expectations and do what you normally do to relax. Read, watch movies, play video games. If checking in with friends over the phone is relaxing, be careful not to get involved in a bunch of negative "what if" questions, which non-competitors have a tendency to ask.

The main goal of the night before is to chill out and relax. Don't dwell on tomorrow. It will come soon enough.

I can't emphasize enough the importance of deliberate control of your thinking—making your mind do what you want it to do. When your emotions are noisy, use planned and rehearsed mental routines to stay poised and balanced, auto mental routines that are no different than a physical pre-shot routine. When it's time to putt, you do x, y, and z. When your emotions are heightened, you do a, b, and c. Both types of routines are repetitive sequences. What are your a, b, and c?

THE MORNING OF

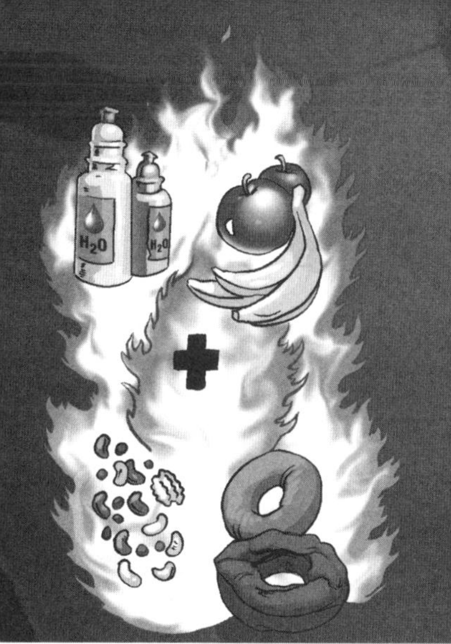

DO

Chill out! There's nothing to do but eat fuel, organize your stuff, and to get ready to head out. Keep occupied with non-golf mental activities.

DON'T

Don't get drawn into Monkey Mode fantasy "what if" scenarios: What if this or what if that, what may or may not happen. The answer is obvious, "who knows." Kick in some LBi.

The Morning Of:

The morning of a tournament is similar to the night before. Stay in chill mode. There's nothing to do but *fuel* well, *organize* your stuff, and get to the course, so mentally and emotionally chill out.

Trick yourself into disengaging from what will be happening within a few hours by giving your mind something positive to do. Stay completely away from any emotional babble of what may or may not happen, what you want to happen, what if this or what if that. All that drama is nothing but a right-brain energy sucker.

You know what wins tournaments, right? One shot. That means there's nothing to do until the first shot. So do something mentally constructive the morning of. Keep your thoughts and feelings focused on what you can believe in, not "what if" hypothetical drama.

If you must think about the round, do some planning, like how and when to take *rest* breaks. This is an important thinking strategy because so few golfers plan when and how they're going to rest.

Knowing when and how to turn your laser-beam focus off is just as important as knowing when and how to turn it on, because staying intensely

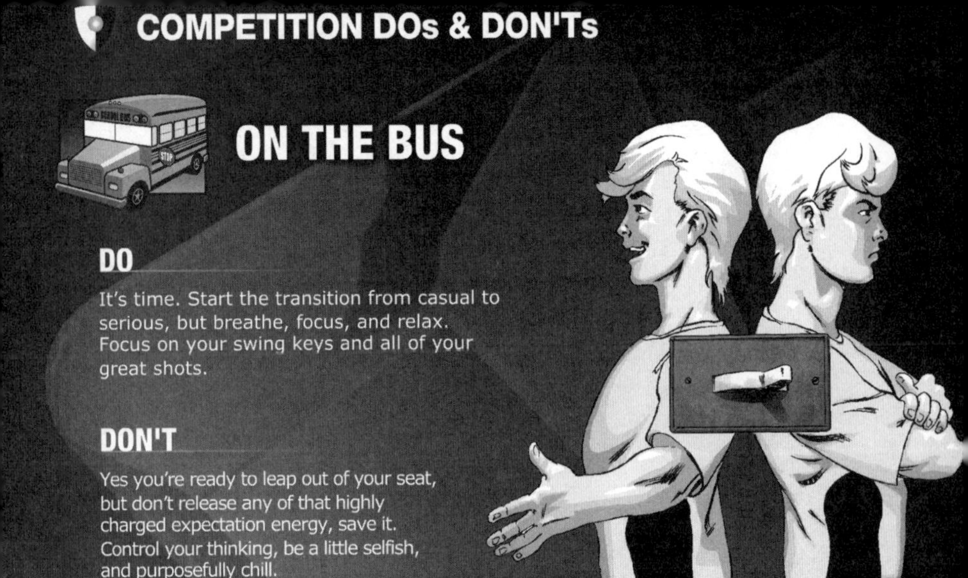

focused all of the time is impossible. If you need to revisit the resting routine in Chapter 2, make a mental note.

The underlying objective of the thinking dos (the morning of a competition) is to chill out and enjoy the moment. Now it's time to get on the bus or jump in the car and head to the course.

On The Bus:

On the bus is just an extension of the morning. Sorta duh, right? There's nothing to do except travel to the course, so chill out. Put on some headphones and get lost in the music. If you're not into music, do what you do to relax.

Your mind and body are ready to compete, your energy is high, but it's not time yet. You must construct ways to purposefully chill out as the storm approaches.

The bus is much more of a challenge than your car. Teammates are great, but they can be very distracting or even worse if they're not mentally competent. Sometimes you can't escape your teammates' energies, so it's very important to figure out how to stay in *your* competition mindset.

If you're the chatty type and that's calming for you, make sure you ride along with a chatty teammate. If you're the quiet type, look for a quiet teammate. Either way, don't let the dynamics of the bus take you out of your comfort zone—do what works best for you.

This is just another aspect of mentally taking control of what needs to be controlled. It's time to *switch,* to be selfish, so do what you need to do to stay in your competition mindset. Just be chill and don't waste energy. Focus not on Little Dog negativity, but on all of your believable Big Dog memories—they are what provide serious personal power.

While traveling to the course, if you need something mentally positive to do, it's a great time to *rehearse*. For example, what do you do mentally after smoking a drive right down the middle? Don't just feel relieved; think about what you did right. What were your swing thoughts? What was the situation? Savor it. You should also rehearse overcoming mistakes. What do you do mentally when you drop a shot? First, don't freak out, beat yourself up, or letdown emotionally. Just like any other negative situation, control it, don't let it control you. Breathe, take charge of your feelings, and let go of that mistake.

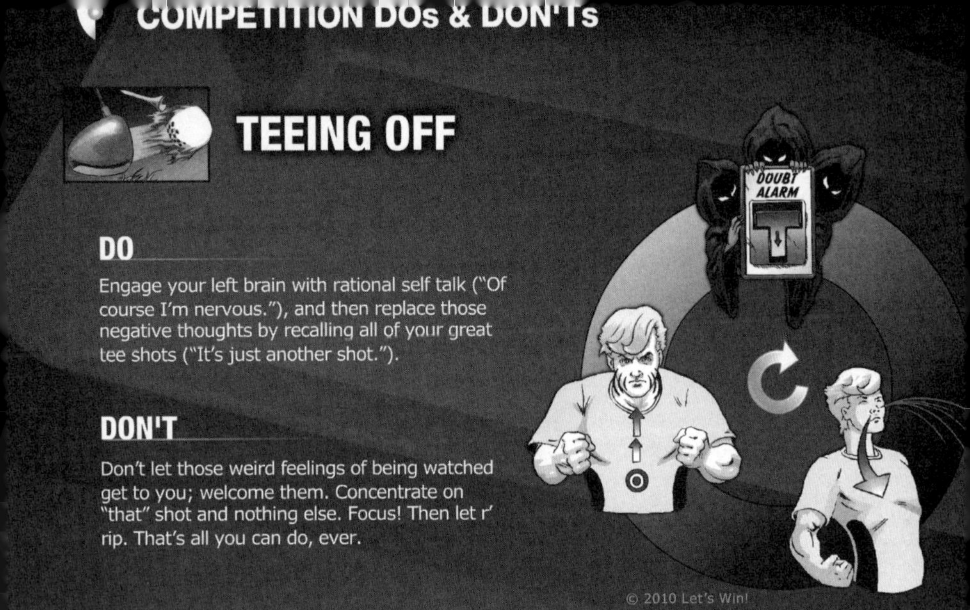

On the bus, or however you travel to the course, is a time to conserve energy by quieting those *expectation* emotions. The focus of the dos is to stay positive; it's just a warm up to controlling your emotions later on, when you're warming up on the driving range or putting green.

The Driving Range:
Now you're in the competitive environment and self-consciousness really kicks in. So many things can be distracting, including spectators. They can either be your best friends or your worst enemies, depending on your mindset. At times, learning how to deal with spectator distractions is a key mental component to controlling *your round.*

Some of us can handle more distractions than others. For example, some people can read effectively in a crowded, noisy room. For me that's impossible. I'm easily distracted, especially by noise. So I tend to narrow my focus as soon as I enter the competitive environment. It's not that I'm antisocial or don't want to support my group or don't like interacting with other competitors, it's because transitions from casual to focused takes me a little more effort. Other competitors can flip the switch and transition

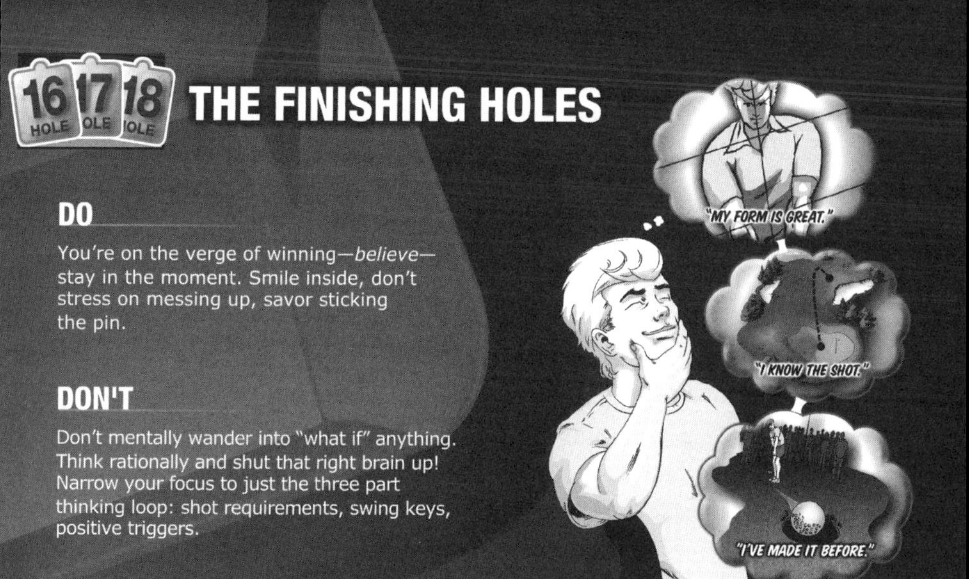

to competition mode in an instant. My mental process is not as quick and requires more concentration.

On the driving range is when you need to seriously *narrow* your concentration to the task at hand, which is quieting your emotions and focusing. Each of us has our own way of transitioning or *switching* from friendly to competitive. What's yours?

The driving range is not only where you narrow and switch to a competition mindset, but also where you *override* any swarming Doubt Demons and *replace* their nonsense with rational thinking. You want to step onto number one filled to the brim with believing, not lost in self-consciousness, distraction, and hesitation.

Teeing Off:

It's show time. Now you're really on stage. You can sense your fellow competitors and the spectators glaring at you from all directions—your mind races with expectations. Remember the *All Eyes On You* illustration from Chapter 2? It's like being in a fishbowl; you're surrounded and there's no escape. Being on display for some is pure horror, while for others it's totally

Believe in your excellent mechanics by drawing on your previous success—quiet down those negative emotions.

cool. Either way, whichever your reaction may be, teeing off under the microscope can be quite the adrenaline rush.

Speaking of adrenaline, let's divert for a bit and talk about adrenaline—powerful stuff. Without getting technical, adrenaline's bottom-line is RUN! When we feel threatened, glands dump adrenaline into our bloodstream, which quickly increases our physical and mental capabilities.

A significant adrenaline rush side-effect to be aware of is that when too much adrenaline is dumped at once, which is usually caused by genuine doubt or extreme fear—our Little Dog is freaking out. A monster adrenaline rush can make us feel nauseated (yep, some puke), lightheaded, unfocused, and physically weak. The aftereffect of a monster adrenaline rush can leave us feeling lethargic and tired—sort of a letdown.

The way out of a monster adrenaline rush is oxygen and concentration; breathe and talk yourself down. Control it, don't let it control you. Use your mental skills to quiet your Little Dog down, so you can mentally get back in the competition.

Back to teeing off—when the announcer calls your name, all eyes are on you. Learn how to let go of that weird awareness of being watched by narrowing your concentration to the shot, the ball, your club, and your swing keys. Focus! Then, let 'er rip. That's all you can do.

Think about it. If you were a golf robot, all of the environmental and emotional distractions would be irrelevant; you wouldn't even notice them. Believing would not be an issue, because as a robot you'd be totally mechanical. A similar example is playing by yourself or with a best friend. When you're not self conscious—you believe and let 'er rip. Just bring that same mindset to competition.

The competition dos to teeing off are focusing on your swing keys and nothing else—absolutely nothing. No "what if" anything. Get all of the "what if" stuff out of the way long before approaching the ball. Gather all the thoughts, memories, and feelings you use to seriously believe, then click into execution mode, pure and simple.

Critical Finishing Holes:

During the critical finishing holes, your true confidence gets tested—your *actual* confidence, not your fantasy confidence. Even though everything is happening at an incredibly fast mental pace, even in golf, it is vital to have the presence of mind to know where you are on the Grr Meter. If you're emotionally tweaked, plug in some LBi and *replace* negative feelings with past success you can believe in. Breathe and focus on your strengths.

Maintaining emotional balance while your mind sees and feels that you're actually close to winning is a unique experience. We see the pros crash on Sunday all of the time. They haven't *looked* into the future and planned how they'll react when they're actually on the verge of winning.

I liken it to giving a class presentation, when you study the information well, but never in your mind walk to the front of the room and turn around and face the class. That's the shocker. When we turn around and see all of those blank faces and judgmental eyes staring straight at us. We study the information, but don't visualize ourselves actually presenting it.

The finishing holes present the same weird type of feedback—we're doing it or we're not, what now? The simple solution is, it's just another golf shot, so repeat the three part thinking loop: shot requirements, swing keys, positive triggers. Dismiss any emotional blah, blah, blah. What tournament? Winning what? It's just a golf shot. Dismiss all of the emotional chatter about winning, no matter what level of a tournament, and execute. Control your emotions by thinking and *believing*, so your body can do what it's trained to do—execute golf shots.

This is why PMA and visualizing victory are not very effective. Saying to yourself "I can, I can, I can," doesn't do much good if your core doesn't believe it. Visualizing victory is worthless if your core is in Little Dog mode dwelling on negative "what if" drama. Consciously controlling your emotions is what enables you to believe and execute shots under the most extreme pressure, which is often felt during the finishing holes.

Remember, it's always about one shot and believing you can make that shot, so dismiss the emotional chatter. The thinking dos are similar for any

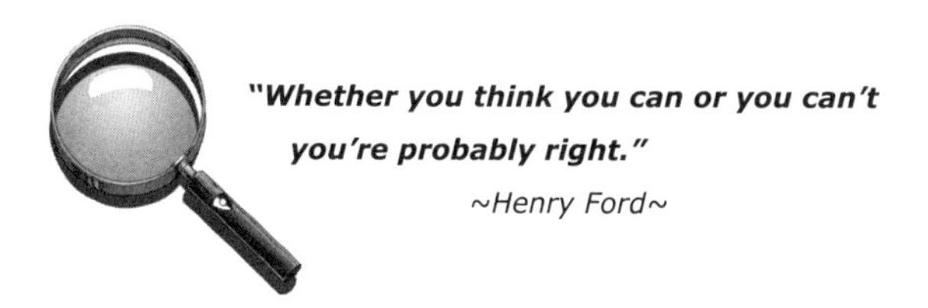

tournament, on any course, in any situation, for any shot. Integrate your left brain, think objectively, believe, and boldly execute.

Deliberate

Since the next chapter is the last, and deals primarily with dedication, discipline, and sacrifice, as I close this chapter, I need to isolate one more term that is key to your success: being deliberate.

Being deliberate in everything you do, with both your swing and your mind is how to succeed in training and in competition. Being deliberate is the absolute opposite of random, haphazard, accidental, disorganized or messy.

Consider the synonyms: purposeful, premeditated, conscious, intentional, calculated, planned, thoughtful, careful, measured, methodical, and the list goes on. Being deliberate is the way to approach everything you do. For example, it took deliberate effort to master a putting stroke without breaking your wrists. It will also take deliberate effort to integrate your left brain to conquer the Demons.

Remember, any tournament situation, let alone a title tournament, will always be a mental and emotional challenge. If you were strapped with a heart-rate indicator and blood-pressure monitor you would be amazed; your heart is pounding and your blood pressure is soaring. This is one reason why I have such a healthy respect for those who love to compete. Staying focused and confidently believing during any competitively threatening situation takes more than guts, it takes *mental toughness* and being deliberate.

Practice and use the skills. Being deliberate and controlling your emotions will lessen the dramatic ups and downs from doubtful to confident; that's how you win the confidence battle. Switch, narrow, fuel, override, replace, and believe—use the skills. Be deliberate and stay with it; force your mind to work. Once you understand and can easily think objectively under pressure, when all eyes are on you, you'll be able to step up and compete with confidence. So Grr up, show some teeth, and let your Big Dog out!

Consider the fact that while others may believe in you, the only believing that matters is you believing in you, so *believe!*

CHAPTER 6

REVIEW

Believe: Let Your Big Dog Out

Summary

The Let's Win! mental toughness skills prepare us to believe in ourselves when it's all on the line. Choosing what to think about effectively neutralizes or seriously reduces debilitating Doubt Demon drama. Use all of the skills to *believe* in yourself when the pressure is on; don't fall victim to a Monkey Mode meltdown.

Test—What did you learn?

True/False Statements:

1) The 3 Doubt Demons don't come back once we defeat them.
2) A competitor's confidence comes from hoping.
3) Our Big Dog self is only interested in facts and rational thought.
4) Believing is a natural result of using all the mental toughness skills.

Do It!

The Doubt Demons use a variety of nonsense to convince you you're not good enough. The next time you are confronted with doubt, fear, or intimidation, recognize it and kick in some LBi thinking. Recall your Big Dog victories by engaging in rational self-talk. Consciously take part in your own achievement by using all the skills. You're good, so believe it and execute.

CHAPTER 7

DREAM

Create **Your Future**

In this chapter you will learn how to *dream*—mental toughness skill #7—a life skill that generates the drive to train hard and sacrifice to excel. Outstanding achievement is accomplished by those few who are motivated, committed, and disciplined.

Our Big Dog self
has a *dream* for our future and
will not make excuses or get lost
pursuing pleasure.

There's only one road to a state or national championship and it's called d-e-d-i-c-a-t-i-o-n. And the road of dedication is paved with discipline, which is why so many athletes come up short—lack of discipline is the champion destroyer. So many great athletes of all ages never come close to achieving their competitive potential, because they haven't created a dream for the future and disciplined themselves to work hard and attain it.

Several years ago, my house was full of teenage athletes, and after watching all of them struggle with discipline, I will be the first to acknowledge that it's tough. Our communities today have few role models representing dedication and discipline. A large portion of America's citizens have grown lazy and unmotivated. Discipline is almost non-existent in our schools and entertainment options are extensive. The cars, cash, contraband, and *extreme socializing* (partying) are constant distractions that prevent personal achievement. I'm not preaching here; I'm cluing you in to what will drag you down.

Every day you're faced with the decision of whether to work or play. Realize that you will progress rapidly in sports and life if you are wise enough to understand that having an eye on the future is what drives success, any kind of success.

Does that make sense? When there is no party to go to, there is no decision to make. That's easy. But when you have options to either train or socialize, *decisions must be made*. Decisions are motivated by having an eye on the future, having something you seriously want, something you're willing to work for, saying "no thanks" to socializing and instead going to work to attain it.

If your desire is to distinguish yourself from the average, to win, to become a champion, you must separate yourself to some degree from the majority of your party peers who are more focused on fun than work. They do not have an eye on the future or the desire to accomplish something special. You do!

While writing *WinningSTATE-FOOTBALL,* I was communicating with Assistant Coach Blaine Davidson of the Bellevue High School Wolverines (Washington state), and at the bottom of his e-mails was the following quote:

> *"The things that failures don't like to do are the very same things that you and I, including the successful, naturally like to do. We have to realize right from the start that success is something achieved by the minority, and is therefore unnatural and not to be achieved by following our natural likes and dislikes, nor by being guided by our natural preferences and prejudices."*
> — Albert Gray.

As that quote expresses so well, you won't see or meet very many people during your lifetime who are genuinely striving to excel and accomplish something extraordinary. Why? It's too scary. The majority of people lack the attitude and motivation (drive) to make courageous decisions. How about you? Can you make decisions that are extraordinary? Decisions that make you different from most people around you? In America today, separating yourself from your party peers in order to train and excel *is* a courageous decision.

Realize that everyone's natural tendencies are to play and have fun, not to work and achieve—let alone to work hard and excel. But to accomplish outstanding feats in the sports arena, we must discipline our natural tendencies by putting them in perspective and managing them. Nike put it best: "Just do it."

The Crossroads illustration (right) vividly presents two paths in life: one that is wholeheartedly dedicated to achievement, and the other that is consumed with pleasure and fun. Which path do you walk? Do you prepare and go train or party and slug out? The choice is clearly yours, along with the consequences.

CHAMPIONVILLE
SLACKERVILLE
© 2010 Let's Win!

Black or White

Even though the work-or-play decision may be fought with extreme anxiety, the outcome is black or white. Either you do or you don't. Either you train or you blow it off. Either you go to class or you don't. Either you study for the test or you don't. At the moment of choice, your mind will play tricks on you. Your Little Dog will present convincing arguments like "you can get away with it just this one time." What an emotional illusion. The heck with your Little Dog—tune into your Big Dog.

For those of us whose temperament is geared more toward work than play, we have an advantage. Personally, I love to practice. I truly enjoy working at getting better at something. For example, after retiring from many years of world-class weight lifting, I was looking for another sport to challenge myself with and found golf. I hit over one hundred balls every day, methodically worked my short game, and played several rounds a week until I achieved a legitimate three handicap. For me, that wasn't a grind, that was fun.

Additionally, those of us who are not overly social have a training advantage. For example, I'm not antisocial, but hanging out and partying has never been compelling to me, even as a teenager. So I've never had to seriously grapple with the work-or-play decision, to train or party. I've always naturally gravitated towards work. I see the decision of whether to go work or go play as being black or white. My inner voice says, "What's your problem? Make the decision. Are you a champion or a slacker?"

My younger son Nick, who was eighteen at the time, was reading the first draft of this chapter and just shook his head and said, "Dad, you still don't get it, you're weird. Most of us don't think like you. For my friends and me, forgetting our friends to go train is like solitary confinement. *It's not a simple decision."*

For many of you the work-or-play battle is intense and fought with extreme anxiety, and you frequently choose your pleasure interests over your achievement interests.

Many of your coaches, especially those who know how to win, will come across with a similar black-or-white mindset—either you do or you don't. But many of you get stuck in the middle, being pulled in both directions. Reconciling this conflict requires perspective, and then disciplined decisions must be made. Remember, this book is not intended to help you feel better about your bad habits—its purpose is to give you the tools to *become* the competitor you have secretly *wished* you were. Hearing the stone-cold truth is how we progress.

So, how do you socialize less and train and mentally prepare more? Here's the bottom line: As an athlete, especially at the young adult level, you can't have it all. An athlete's commitments are triple those of most non-athletes. There just isn't enough time to get everything in, and getting consistent sleep is the main problem.

Consistent, deep rest is crucial for athletes. We train, practice hard, lift weights, and condition. The only way to recover and regenerate is through premium fueling and consistent, deep sleep. Partying and hanging out cut into sleep and can be devastating distractions. You have to get up at six or seven in the morning to go to school—or even earlier to work out before school—while your party friends are snug and warm, snoring in their beds. They have nothing to get up for except the next party. You're different.

Do you have the courage to be exceptional? Do you want/need to win so bad that you get goose bumps? If you sincerely want to excel, if it truly is a burning desire in your gut, you must make disciplined black-or-white decisions that are *driven by your dream.*

Disciplined Decisions

Performing at a high level requires balance—that's the challenge. A balanced daily schedule requires conscious, focused, disciplined decisions and actions. There's no way around it.

Let's consider the definition of **dis-ci-pline**: "activity or exercise that develops or improves a skill."

If you don't have a love-to-practice temperament like I do, then discipline is not about fun, it's about work. Being genuinely disciplined is a rigorous, moment-by-moment task. What helps the decision process is knowing why you're doing what you're doing and why nothing will get in your way of achieving it—*absolutely nothing.* Then it's much easier to say "no thanks" to the constant barrage of social distractions, drag yourself off the couch, and get to work.

Does this mean you shouldn't have a social life? Not at all! It's about balance. If you were talking to a pro golfer you respect, and he was asking you about your dreams and goals for golf and how much practice you put in, what would you say? "Only enough that it doesn't get in the way of my socializing"? How do you think he would respond?

It's okay to hang out with friends a bit and blow off some steam. But be deliberate and know what you're doing. Don't get lost in the party moment. You're not a mindless pleasure seeker, you're an athlete/competitor seriously wanting to win.

Competing at a high level takes a greater commitment than the average person is willing to put in. That commitment means being as disciplined as possible while not becoming a stranger to your friends and family.

I've known and watched so many great athletes fail because they were unable to give up fun for training. I've also known and watched numerous successful athletes who were smart enough to figure out how to get in some time to hang out without disrupting their training schedule. In fact, I know of highly successful athletes who purposefully schedule in that time to break up training and to give themselves a break. But they do it with purpose, not training avoidance.

Balance is the key, and if you have lots of entertainment options, which most of you do, disciplined decisions are required. Your dream, supported by tangible goals, is what drives winning decisions. So don't be a slacker, dedicate yourself to achieving your dream. Make decisions that propel you toward becoming the complete athlete.

CHAMPION VS. SLACKER

Dream big and dedicate yourself to achieving.

Time	Champion	Slacker
6:15	Thirty minute run	Sleep
7:15	Fuel	Still sleeping
7:50	School	Still sleeping - skip school
12:30	Fuel	Junk food
1:10	Weight training	Smoke dope
2:50	Practice	Video games
5:30	Fuel	Junk food
6:00	Home work	Smoke more dope
7:00	Hang-out	Hang-out
9:45	MT Training	Hang-out
10:00	Lights out	Party time

DAILY SCHEDULE

Dream vs. Goals

Let's separate a dream from a goal. A dream is not a goal. Goals are short term markers that we use as targets on the way to accomplishing our dream. Our dream is more about what we're going to get from the goals, dedication, hard work, and personal sacrifice. Too often we only focus on goals, which tend to be bland and tasteless.

Your dream should be full of emotions, feelings, and glory. Your dream must be so big and real that you can taste it. When you think about your dream, it should make your mouth water and the hair on the back of your neck stand up. Thinking about your dream should move the Grr Meter in the plus direction—it should deeply motivate you.

This is where many of you get lost in the present. You don't create a vision of the future for yourself. It's so important to picture the future. Don't give in to the short-term pursuit of pleasure, social indulgence, or laziness.

Consider this: Is the desire to be a champion a goal or a dream? It's a dream. A goal is being able to drive the ball 290 yards, hit fifteen out of eighteen greens, or spend an hour on the putting green five days a week.

All the things you'll get by accomplishing those goals and winning the title tournament are what drives the dream. Ink in the local paper, maybe even some national press, a scholarship, showing yourself you really can do something significant when you put your mind to it, distinguishing yourself as a champion—all those things set a tone for the rest of your life, and the list goes on.

There are many examples of what one gets from achieving a big dream, but what's most important is for you to create your list of what you'll get from achieving your dream.

Example: Respond to these questions: "If I won ..., I would get ...," "If I won ..., I would be able to...." Answering those questions in detail has a forward-looking perspective and produces mental pictures and feelings associated with that potential achievement.

Here's another example. When you wanted your first car so bad it hurt, why was that desire so intense? Because you had tons of mental pictures and feelings of what it would be like to have a car: feeling cool, being free, dating, and running around with your friends. Those feelings that went along with the thoughts of having a car were the core of your *car dream.* Then, you set a series of goals to get the car to live the dream.

Your dream drives the motivation, which leads to setting goals, which leads to achieving your dream. Make sense?

A dream that you can taste, that you can believe you can achieve, is what motivates you to set goals and then to do the work to reach those goals. Find your motivation by creating a dream and knowing clearly what you want from accomplishing your dream.

Find Your Motivation

So many of you struggle with doing what is necessary and giving it your all, every single day. Some days you're on and some days you're off. Some days you have a dream and its motivating force, but most days you don't. Okay, yeah, it's fun to socialize, but what do you gain from it other than relationship building and immediate gratification? Answer: Nothing that will make you a better competitor or a champion. When you're feeling lazy and would rather blow off training and do nothing, what fires you up to take yourself

DREAM

MENTAL SKILL #7: Dream big; your success demands it.

Strong Dreams

I want to go to college and need a scholarship.

I want to prove to myself and everyone else that I can be great at something.

I want to distinguish myself as a person who can strive, persevere, and achieve.

I want to be a pro athlete and make a living doing what I love.

Non-Dreams

It's something to do.

I have friends on the team.

My mom or dad was an athlete.

Coach says, "You could be really good."

***Dream**—mental skill #7.* Without a strong dream to strive for, how can you expect yourself to sacrifice and train hard day in and day out? You can't. Our fire, our passion comes from wanting to achieve, so learn how to dream big, nothing is holding you back, but you.

by the ear and get to work? Yep, a real dream, one that you must accomplish for your life to feel complete.

Find your motivation. Why are you out for your sport? Why are you putting yourself through the long practices and social isolation? If it's just to do something or to hang with your athlete friends, that's okay, but you'll probably lack motivation to excel. When you have a dream, you have the drive to make disciplined decisions to train rather than play. When you train more, typically the outcome is better. Without a dream, your core motivation, your fire, is dull and weak.

How much fire do you have to achieve? Is it weak or powerful? How much heart do you have to push forward and train when your friends are giving up? Do you have the courage to strive for excellence? Ask yourself those questions and answer them truthfully. Then feel your commitment and dedication grow.

I hope I'm expressing this achievement point with maximum clarity. You need a dream to be able to say "no thanks" to the social opportunities that present themselves every day and to overcome laziness so you can train and prepare. The clarity of your dream is what helps you stay dedicated. If you don't have a real dream driving your desire to excel, and if the reasons why you want to achieve aren't *crystal clear,* then staying committed will be a tremendous challenge—if you can stay committed at all. Your dream is your emotional power. A car dream is crystal clear, vivid, and tangible. Your sports dream must have the same clarity.

Here are some weak, no-dream examples:
1) It's something to do;
2) You have friends on the team;
3) Your Mom or Dad was an athlete;
4) Coach says, "You could be really good."

Here are some strong big-dream examples:
1) You want to go to college and you need a scholarship;
2) You want to prove to yourself and everyone else that you can be great at something;
3) You want to distinguish yourself as a person who can strive, persevere, and achieve;
4) You want to be a pro athlete and make a living at what you love.

Once you think about it, even a little, there are many other examples of strong dreams. It is absolutely vital that you have a clear, vivid vision of your dream, and yes, every day it will be a battle—entertainment and lying-on-the-couch options require disciplined decisions. Again, most Americans don't make courageous decisions to forsake immediate pleasure for long-term personal achievement.

Here's what you might be thinking, "I have a dream, but I still struggle with dedication and discipline." I know many of you feel that way. The missing ingredient is sacrifice.

Sacrifice

If you do have a dream, want it really bad, and are motivated to get it, you might be thinking, "When I put this book down, I'm gonna go make things happen." But for those of you who are still being pulled in both directions, you must take hold of the *fact* that dedication and discipline require sacrificing. It's just the way it is.

Part of the quote from the football coach's email, "success is something achieved by the minority," really says it all. In order to be a champion at anything, you have to do things which elevate you above the average, things which require sacrifice. **Sac-ri-fice**: "the surrender of something valued for the sake of something having a higher or more pressing claim."

When you really want something bad, nothing gets in your way, right? And you sacrifice things to get what you want.

A simpler definition of sacrifice is "less party and more work equals achievement." Saying "no thanks" to social invitations, or calling it a night long before others do, is surrendering something valued—time with your friends. No dream, no surrender. You have to *submit* to the reality of striving for excellence. The bottom line is you can't have it all. It's just the way

"In reading the lives of great men, I found that the first victory they won was over themselves ...self-discipline with all of them came first."

~Harry S. Truman~

Dream big and commit. Your motivation and emotional power depend on it, and your success demands it!

it is. And when you do commit and sacrifice, you will get everything in return—things most people only fantasize about as they never take action or sacrifice to get them.

Most who resist committing and sacrificing usually don't accomplish much. Realize that commitment and sacrifice are key differences between becoming a champion and staying a contender. You, a champion, will submit yourself to the sacrifices of training, realizing that in order to acquire success—the results of a dream—sacrifices must be made.

Here's a story of no sacrifice. Several years ago, I mentored a high school senior who was a gifted athlete, physically. He played a variety of sports from the time he could walk. Football and basketball ended up being his two primary interests.

When he got to high school, he was heading down the party road and by his sophomore year was pretty much self-destructing. His junior year was a disaster; academically he was a no-show, and of course he was not eligible for sports.

He had been a good friend of my son Nick since grammar school, and the summer before his senior year we ran into him. After sharing his personal story, we offered to take him in, hoping that a fresh start and new environment would help him get back on track to finish high school and ultimately to go to college.

At first, he was negative and reluctant. He thought he was too far behind—besides, there was no guarantee he would be eligible to play sports. I told him that to assume things in life is, well, ignorant and suggested that with a couple of investigative phone calls he would know exactly what his options were. He agreed, and within a couple of calls found out that he could enroll and was eligible. He moved in with us, agreeing to my one condition—he had to go to school, no excuses. If he didn't, he'd have to move out.

He was pumped. He was back in school and on the football field again. Practice went great and he quickly earned a starting position at corner. He contributed in the first couple of games and was looking forward to a great season. Then the phone call came.

I thought I had kept in pretty close contact with him regarding attendance and what I heard was, "Are you kidding, I'm going to every class. Why would I blow this?"

He lied. The athletic director told me he had been skipping class since the first day of school. His attendance record was barely 50%.

Unfortunately, I had to ask him to move out. To keep up his end of the deal, all that he had to do was go to class. There were no grade requirements. *Just go to class.*

So don't be a slacker, dedicate yourself to achieving your dream. Make decisions that propel you toward becoming the complete athlete.

As I was discussing with him why he chose to skip school and blow the opportunity, he looked at me like I was some sort of idiot and said, "Because I want to have fun."

I'll never forget that—fun, at the expense of everything.

For whatever reason, it was more important for this young man to identify, connect with, and relate to kids who were consumed with socializing and partying than the kids who wanted to achieve and excel. At the time, he made undisciplined decisions and had to suffer the consequences.

If you're wondering why I didn't tell you an overcoming-the-obstacles, pump-you-up kind of story, it's because you hear those kinds of stories all of the time. It's like the Navy Seal example; recruits don't get sent to inspiration school to learn how to overcome fear and intimidation, they get sent to learn-how-to-think school. Inspiring stories are cool, but they don't get at the reality of issue, which is if you don't commit and sacrifice, you will not excel.

Trust me, dedication, discipline, and sacrifice have to be your best friends if you want to succeed—at anything.

The Moment Of Temptation

Over the course of the season, you'll be confronted many times with "do you" or "don't you" decisions. Do you get up and go to school or sleep in? Do you follow through with scheduled mental preparation or blow it off and hang out? Do you stay out late and party or go home and rest up for tomorrow's training? Each decision is a *test*, to slack off or get it done, to succumb to temptation or Grr up and fight back.

Your party friends will provide added pressure, "Come on, just hang out with us, you train all of the time." And of course you'll want to, which isn't a bad thing—you're human. But each time you let the temptation of partying and laziness cut into your training and preparation you're jeopardizing your potential. Your Little Dog will try to convince you that you've trained enough.

Muster the courage to quiet your Little Dog down by letting your Big Dog out; you're on a journey to become a unique member of our championship community—those who can overcome temptation and are willing to submit to the sacrifices required for higher achievements.

No doubt your decision record won't be perfect when the season is over. That's okay, perfection is not the goal. *Trying is the goal.* Make more positive decisions than negative. Make more decisions that propel you toward outstanding achievement than decisions that trap you among the average, and mediocrity.

The Schedule

Once you envision a real dream and decide with conviction that you can sacrifice daily social outings by separating yourself somewhat from the pleasure pack, I strongly recommend that you put together a daily/weekly schedule. Give yourself a framework to operate in. It can be as detailed as you like, which depends on your personality type. But give yourself a daily/weekly outline of what you *need* to do, along with what you *want* to do. Set daily and weekly goals to achieve something significant, and do it.

Photo: The University of West Florida celebrates their victory during the final round of the Division II Men's Golf Championship held at Memorial Park Golf Course in Houston, TX. *Dave Einsel/NCAA Photos*

WF
NCAA
NATIONAL CHAMPION

If you just take a little time to plan, you will still be able to schedule in some time to hang out, just not as much as your party friends. That's why you'll be competitive and victorious and set yourself above the rest. It truly is your decision.

110% Effort

Notice that I haven't even mentioned "give it your all." Give everything you do 110% percent—go, go, go, and go some more.

Intensity of effort is another deal. That comes from your personal drive, your Big Dog factor.

Personally, I would rather see athletes give 90% effort 100% of the time than see athletes give 110% effort 80% of the time. The great champions, of course, give 110% every single moment. What about you?

Dream Big

Without a vivid picture of a real dream, it doesn't matter who tries to push you—you won't have the burning desire to make the difficult decisions that confront you every day.

Grasp the opportunity to better yourself by creating an achievable dream and then committing to the dedication, discipline, and sacrifice required to accomplish it.

Sam Huff said, "Discipline is the key to being successful. We all get twenty-four hours a day. It's up to us what we do with those twenty-four hours."

You've only got one life. Your future is yours and yours only, so dream big and commit—your motivation and emotional power depend on it, and your success demands it!

CHAPTER 7

REVIEW

Dream: Create Your Future

Summary

Real achievement doesn't automatically happen, it requires extraordinary effort. The kind of effort very few are willing to put in. Becoming a champion—winning *anything* significant—requires dedication, discipline, and sacrifice. The drive to train hard day in and day out comes from having a tangible *dream*, not from goals. What's your dream?

Test—What did you learn?

True/False:

1) Champions never get to socialize.
2) There is no difference between a goal and a dream.
3) Dedication, discipline, and sacrifice have to be your best friends if you want to succeed—at anything.
4) Joining the championship club of achievers requires only putting in the amount of time that doesn't take away from having fun.

Do It!

Identify your dream. Write it down. Clearly envision the glory—what you're going to get once you achieve your dream. Then, and this is the most important thing, commit! Day by day, one decision at a time, make it happen. Your social life and your lazy factor will provide tons of obstacles. Be brave; make courageous disciplined decisions, so you can become part of our unique community of achievers.

EXPECTATIONS

What to expect:

Now, you can actually *do* something to mentally prepare for competition. Under pressure, you can expect to be less anxious and more rational, which translates into having greater emotional control and increased confidence. You can expect your new competition insights and mental toughness skills to give you a greater sense of control and a powerful, bold, assertive feeling at your core—a Big Dog competition mindset.

What not to expect:

Similar to the first time you went to a driving range and didn't leave with a perfect swing, don't expect a complete mental toughness makeover in one read. Think. Be realistic—mental toughness skills are about logic, not emotion. Overcoming primal doubting and distracted thinking will require some serious mental effort, so let's dig in and get to work.

Do it:

Life, every day, is your practice arena; you have unlimited opportunities to practice and improve—just use the skills to engage your logical brain and think. Be patient. Self-reflection and attitude adjustments are not simple. Push yourself to the edge of your comfort zone to increase your ability to use the skills under pressure. *Think logically* about why you can make the shot, and when you believe it, you will.

CHAPTER REVIEW TEST ANSWERS

1) **Switching to a competition mindset is essential: TRUE.**
   Deliberately *switching* your attitude from friendly and agreeable to challenging and assertive is essential. Why? Competing is not like our social life, relaxed and comfortable; competing is aggressive and on edge.

2) **Successful competitors float between -1 and +1 on the Grr Meter: TRUE.**
   Competing is harsh, rough, and intense, but too much Grr is just as confusing and distracting a too little. Successful competitors balance their emotions.

3) **The Doubt Demon of Fear is one of the 3 Doubt Demons: FALSE.**
   The 3 Doubt Demons are the Demon of Embarrassment, the Demon of Inadequacy,

and the Demon of Past Failure. They plot and plan to make us feel small, fearful, and intimidated.

4) **Our left brain controls our emotions: FALSE.**
   Our right brain controls our emotions and Monkey Mode behavior. By increasing our left-brain dominance, we lessen the intensity of our right-brain drama, replacing emotional chaos with rational stability.

1) **We block out distractions by narrowing our focus to something positive: TRUE.**
   We use the PRE Competition Routines to mentally prepare for the emotional drama and doubtful thinking that will always accompany pressure situations—always. We narrow our focus to stay balanced and positive when it's all on the line.
2) **Narrowing our concentration helps reduce emotional chaos: TRUE.**
   The Battle Zones familiarity technique helps us mentally deal with the *unfamiliar* aspects at any course by narrowing our concentration to the *familiar* aspects of every course, which helps reduce the emotional drama.
3) **Making it to a title tournament means it's time to celebrate: FALSE.**
   Absolutely not! Don't blow it once you get to state or an important title tournament by over-socializing and fooling around.
4) **Periodically resting the mind is essential to maintaining concentration over long hours: TRUE.**
   When competing, resting is more for your mind than it is for your body, and it is essential to maintaining concentration over long hours. Construct a rest routine.

1) **Premium sources of fuel come from nature and are not processed: TRUE.**
   Premium sources of food and fluids have not been processed or modified from their original states—they come from nature. Nature provides premium high-performance fuel. Machines provide processed tongue food, not mind-and-body fuel.
2) **Competitors should eat lots of proteins the day of a competition: FALSE.**
   On tournament day, proteins are not premium energy sources. Proteins are like wet logs on a fire—they don't burn quickly.
3) **Refined sugar (candy, soda pop, honey, etc.) is a great source of carbs: FALSE.**
   Sugary foods and fluids have absolutely no place in a focused, Big Dog competitor's diet—at all, ever! Get off the sugar rollercoaster.
4) **Competitors should avoid all fats during competition: FALSE.**
   Fats are the most important *fuel* for your competitive fire. Your body loves fat because it's concentrated, dense energy. Fats are the large, dry logs for your body's furnace.

OVERRIDE

1) **The 3 Doubt Demons are detectable: TRUE.**
   Yes, detecting doubt is as simple as identifying any other emotion. It requires being emotional intelligent and laughing it off, while rationally talking yourself down with LBi skills.
2) **Your level of confidence is only determined by your genetics: FALSE.**
   Many factors determine our level of confidence, and to be clutch competitors we must learn to surpass our genetics and upbringing influences. We must fight back and control our emotions in order to excel.
3) **Shy, timid athletes can never be assertive, confident competitors: FALSE.**
   That is absolutely false. Just because we're small or naturally more timid does not prevent us from being fierce, dominant competitors—*attitude is a choice.*
4) **Mental toughness has nothing to do with self-reflection: FALSE.**
   Mental toughness definitely includes grappling with self-reflection—how one views oneself. Gaining insight into your competitive self is powerful, because you can then work on the competitor you want to become.

REPLACE

1) **A Big Dog moment is only when we win the trophy: FALSE.**
   A Big Dog moment is about winning *inside*—overcoming our hesitant reactions. A Big Dog moment is when we face an emotional challenge, Grr up, and submit our Demons, when we push forward and execute. There's no Big Dog moment without serious pressure—real intimidation—followed by recovery and execution.
2) **LBi thinking is a repetition of positive statements: FALSE.**
   LBi thinking is much more than PMA. Left-brain-integrated thinking is based on believable memories, not fantasies and hype.
3) **Our emotional right brain has a very loud voice: TRUE.**
   Our two minds are constantly battling for control or, in many cases, not battling due to our Little Dog self having already won. Our emotional right brain has a very loud voice and for most, it is the dominant voice.
4) **Weighting our Memory Scale positive is essential: TRUE.**
   Yes, definitely. Your core confidence is based on *you believing in you.* That belief is based on whether you remember more positive than negative.

BELIEVE

1) **The 3 Doubt Demons don't come back once we defeat them: FALSE**

   The 3 Doubt Demons are relentless. They constantly push our buttons attempting to convince us that we don't have what it takes.

2) **A competitor's confidence comes from hoping: FALSE.**

   A competitor's confidence definitely comes from thinking rationally and drawing on previous success.

3) **Our Big Dog self is only interested in facts and rational thought: TRUE.**

   Your Big Dog is only interested in the facts and actual events, not emotional "what if" drama.

4) **Believing is a natural result of using all the mental toughness skills: TRUE.**

   Solid execution comes from believing, and believing comes from using all the skills to think and choose. Believing in yourself under pressure requires *choosing* what to think about. Yes, choosing, rather than just emotionally reacting.

DREAM

1) **Champions never get to socialize: FALSE.**

   It's about balance. Smart competitors figure out how to get in some time to hang out while not disrupting their training schedule.

2) **There is no difference between a goal and a dream: FALSE.**

   A dream is not a goal. Goals are short-term markers we use as targets on the way to accomplishing our dream.

3) **Dedication, discipline, and sacrifice have to be your best friends if you want to succeed—at anything: TRUE.**

   Absolutely! Dedication, discipline, and sacrifice will have to be your best friends if you want to succeed—at anything.

4) **Joining the championship club of achievers requires only putting in enough time that doesn't take away from having fun: FALSE.**

   Training and preparation require what they require. Each time you let partying/laziness cut into your training/preparation, you jeopardize becoming a member of our championship community—those who will submit to the sacrifices required for higher achievements.